O9-AID-942

THE
FORCE OF
FINANCE

History: The Human Gamble
(University of Chicago Press, 1983)
Betting on Ideas: Wars, Invention, Inflation
(University of Chicago Press, 1985)
Rivalry: In Business, Science, among Nations
(Cambridge University Press, 1989)
*Gambling and Speculation: A Theory, a History and a Future
of Some Human Decisions*
(with Gabrielle A. Brenner; Cambridge University Press, 1990)
Educating Economists
(with David Colander; University of Michigan Press, 1992)
Labyrinths of Prosperity: Economic Follies, Democratic Remedies
(University of Michigan Press, 1994)

THE
FORCE OF
FINANCE

TRIUMPH OF THE CAPITAL MARKETS

REUVEN BRENNER

TEXERE
New York • London

To my wife, Gabrielle,
who stood by me through fire and water,
literally speaking

CONTENTS

ACKNOWLEDGMENTS

I am grateful to the many people who have commented on the chapters of this book in their earlier incarnations as speeches and articles. Here is a list from memory: Martin Anderson, David Asman, Arnold Beichman, David Boaz, Don Chew, David Colander, Robert Conquest, Robert Darton, Milton Friedman, David Goldman, Steve Hanke, Joseph Livni, Henry Manne, William McNeill, Laury Minard, Joel Mokyr, Robert Mundell, Anna Schwartz, Judy Shelton, Paul Volcker, Jude Wanniski, and James Wilson. I apologize to those whose names I have inadvertently skipped.

I am also grateful for the wonderful editing of Don Bastian and Janice Weaver, and for the most intelligent indexing of Gillian Watts. I also thank the staff of my Canadian publisher – Siobhan Blessing in particular, for her meticulous supervision. But special thanks must go to Angel Guerra, who took the initiative of convincing me to put this book together. I mean this sincerely, I had absolutely no intention of writing another book. Angel knew how to touch the soft spots.

Early versions of material in this book were published in journals and magazines, among them *Forbes, Forbes Global, National Post, Dow Jones' Markets, The Wall Street Journal, Strait Times, Journal of Applied Corporate Finance, Jobs and Capital, The International Economy, Cato Policy Report,* and *Queen's Quarterly.* Some were also reprinted on the Web sites MetaMarkets.com, Polyconomics.com, and others.

Preface to the U.S. and International Edition

The Canadian edition appeared under the title *The Financial Century*.

- What is the link between financial markets and betting on extreme ideas, religious, political or other?
- Why has there always been a clear relationship between political instability and either the prohibition of, or weakening of, capital markets within countries? How and why do moves toward democratized capital markets provide stabilizing solutions?
- Why haven't many of the much-anticipated beneficial effects of faster movement of information, capital and people during the last decade—that define "globalization"—been realized? What went wrong—and, more importantly—what are the solutions?
- And how are these solutions hindered today by the delegation of

"financial analyses," of "economics" and "political science," of "sociology" to narrowly specialized "experts"? Why does the subsequent invention of jargon bias thoughts, leading to disastrous policies?

• Can an understanding through history and signals offered by financial markets—using plain language and avoiding the jargon drawing on religious and academic traditions—provide better solutions than these "experts"? The historian Friedrich Heer gave the positive answer to this question years ago when he wrote, "all intellectual discussions . . . are struggles for language." He furiously attacked the fashions of his days—still dominating currently—of playing with and inventing words, rather than using plain language with precision to both analyze and come up with solutions.

• The United States is currently pursuing peace and military victory and, with this long-term objective, prosperity is being defended. But what does "victory" mean? The answer I found was that enduring evidence of victory comes with the democratization of capital markets around the world.

Thus, the questions and issues I addressed in this book turned out to be timeless and timely.

Greek legend spoke about the Phoenix, a fabulous bird sacred to the Egyptians that enriched the country. The bird then sang a melodious dirge, flapped its wings to set the accumulated wealth and itself afire, and rose from the ashes with new, vigorous life.

The metaphor reveals a fundamental trait of human nature following tragedy, whether wars, disasters, corporate bankruptcy or national default. When push comes to shove, people abandon traditions, they bet on new ideas and they sustain heightened levels of effort. Whether the response—the higher levels of efforts—goes into constructive or destructive directions, depends on where these efforts are channeled. In countries with no financial markets to speak of, and with little political accountability, the efforts become destructive. These countries do not rise from the ashes. They fall behind, becoming mired in tribal and ethnic fights, and in petty envy. Ideas and efforts become expressed in religious, racist, messianic or nationalist fervors that have destabilizing effects on the entire world.

Countries that move toward opening up financial markets, instituting more checks and balances in their political sphere, and democratizing politics, soar on more solid foundations. Democratized financial markets and greater accountability in both private and political spheres allow people to start anew and take chances on a variety of imagined futures, chances that, more often than not, go into constructive directions.

In societies where people have no access to capital, they cannot bet on many futures because they get stuck with one "official" future—the one imagined by the political power, who is the only source of finance. These societies stay buried in the past, fall behind and become frustratingly obsessed with drawing up the balance sheets of history. The closed society—and the relatively small role business plays in it—shapes customs and habits of mind that have long-term—very long-term—consequences.

Already in Ancient Greece, financial documents reflected the use of arithmetic when dealing with taxes, debts, division of profits and inheritances, determination of commissions, and negative numbers made their first appearance interpreted as debts. Though much of this knowledge fell into oblivion in Western Europe until the eleventh century, it was kept alive under Islam. Islam represented civilization and commerce thrived in its sphere, while Western Europeans were simply " barbarians at the gate."

Starting in the eleventh century and carrying on through the twelveth century, the roles are reversed. Western Europe moves toward separating State and Church, which had the unintended consequence for the trading classes to obtain rights of paying less taxes, of controlling how much rulers could spend in particular and pursuing ventures. Countries, including Spain under the Inquisition, that did not separate church and state fell behind. The lack of competition in the political sphere prevented financial markets and commercial classes from rising and shaped habits of mind.

Open—and closed—financial markets and the resulting difference in commercialization shape long term habits of mind. The greater the role of business , the more transactions there are, and the greater are the pressures to express all values in terms of a standard—call it "money"—and measure all contracts in its terms. To describe what these transactions are, and how to price them, is far from a trivial exercise. Prices—present values of goods to be delivered in the future in particular—will be approximations, reflecting probabilities and expectations. Because of difficulties in fulfillment when pricing uncertain quantities, price becomes just one feature of a complex contractual agreement. As societies become more commercial and arithmetic, discussions about probability and risk develop. Simultaneously, the increased complexity of contracts requires heightened legal reasoning and institutions backing them. And the contrary: preoccupations about risk and contracts stay negligible in societies where financial markets were never allowed to exist, and securitization could not develop.

With this outlook on life getting hold on people's imagination, James Franklin remarks in his Science of Conjecture, "in Islamic law, the idea of contracts involving risk survived but only for the purpose of prohibiting them." Franklin adds: "The Prophet forbade games of chance and, according to authoritative traditions, also any contract that involved gharar—any risk, uncertainty, or speculation." Under Islam, people could not sell rights to shoot birds in the air even if it was expected that these birds return to their nest. Neither could they sell future crops, or fish in the water—unless its catching was certain because the water was shallow and the water belonged to the vendor. Briefly, in places that did not go through separation of powers, Church and State in particular, religion becomes "fundamental": God can't be wrong. And there is no point discussing "risk."

In all Islamic states, except Turkey in the twentieth century, the lack of separation of powers has resulted in accepting interpretations of the Koran as final arbiters on commercial and financial matters, debates falling into oblivion. In sharp contrast, European

Christian scholars moved in the 11th century to rediscover Greek and Islam classics and focused their discussion on risk, probabilities, contracts and "reason."

Religion may offer a moral compass, but does not offer solution to practical problems societies are facing, in particular when their populations are exploding. Unfortunately stumbling on natural riches, only makes matters far worse in countries—Latin American and African among them—where there is no separation of powers. The rents those in power get for these riches give momentary illusions of prosperity, strengthen the hands of those in power, slow down the democratizing process, and the opening of their financial markets.

Worse: finding the "manna in the ground" is interpreted as Divine favoritism. It allows members of particular society to enjoy the fruits of another civilization, without hard work. Stumbling on natural treasures has this effect—and not only in the Middle East, with its vast oil riches— because those in power can both spend more on the military and distribute part of the rents, bribing sufficient number of people into obedience and flattery. Problems start when it is suddenly realized that such rents do not last forever. Once the price of the natural resources drops, there is less to redistribute and keep people in check. The government or the monarch can redistribute less, reduce the military (their number, their wages or both), and they can no longer enforce the traditional order. The sudden falling behind leads to a rude awakening and often, a coup d'etat. This leapfrogging process has—and always had—dangerous unpredictable consequences.

Mark Twain was right: history does not repeat itself, but it rhymes. The rhyme concerns clashes between societies. Where State and Church were separated (or where there were other competing powers) civilizations thrived; where there were no competing powers in the political sphere, countries' economies withered. The problem is not any particular religion, but rather the lack of separation of powers. The victorious political monopoly prevents the development of commercial, stabilizing middle classes. Those in power always understand that nothing disperses their power more than open capital markets which is why they prohibit and regulate the markets, ensuring that people depend on them. Such dependence brings about passivity and obedience among the population, since obedience guarantees if not a good life, at least a safe one. The powers that be are happy to subsidize and spread teachings to rationalize such attitudes.

Indeed, even if the separation of powers existed, but financial markets were either weakened or destroyed—as happened in Western Europe after World War I—, significant fractions escaped into "certainties"—nationalist, racist or communist—and the jargon of these ideologies replaced the religious one. Since weakened financial markets put societies at a disadvantage, the search for scapegoats was never far behind, and both politicians and obliging priesthood and "intellectuals" came up quickly inventing imaginary enemies. The new leadership promised to destroy them—the Jews, the "kulaks," the "capitalists," the "infidels," "the U.S.," take your pick—since they were the obstacles to shaping the "perfect" society.

Which brings us back to examine the possible of effects of destruction of life and property such as happen after wars, terrorist attacks or natural disasters.

When Philip II's gold-endowed Spain fought the seemingly poor Dutch, the latter not only won the war but became the economic miracle of the seventeenth century—in spite of the fact that they had to overcome the natural obstacle of much of their land being under sea-level too. How? The Dutch created the first federal state in Europe, which was tolerant of all religious groups, and they created the first stock market in the world too, where sophisticated derivatives were traded, and which attracted financiers and skilled craftsmen from the rest of Europe, Russia and India.

After the Second World War, the Jewish survivors in Europe who landed in countries with open capital markets thrived, despite losing their families and everything else. Those who found themselves under Communism did not succeed—until they were allowed to leave for the West or Israel. Israel's emergence on the commercial-high-tech map, becoming within ten years the country with the third largest number of companies listed on NASDAQ (following the U.S. and Canada), is due to the influx of a few hundred thousand highly trained Russian immigrants, and the rapid deregulation of its financial markets.

The Shanghai-based Chinese, their property destroyed and confiscated, similarly rose from the ashes in Hong Kong. The Chinese thrown out of Malaysia flourished in Singapore. Loss of family and property—tragic as they are—do not condemn people to poverty. People are condemned to poverty when political powers keep capital markets closed, thus denying people access to borrow against futures they would like to bet on.

Consider Germany after World War II: much of its infrastructure was in shambles and millions of lives were lost. Still, West Germany revived rapidly and communist East Germany did not. Germany recovered not so much because of the Marshall Plan, generous as that plan was, but because Ludwig Erhard, Germany's finance minister, carried out a drastic currency reform and severe tax cuts; Germany saw the influx of millions of skilled immigrants from Poland, Czechoslovakia and East Germany.

Crises quickly bring people back to fundamentals. The United States recovered rapidly from the Cuban Missile Crisis, the Kennedy assassination, and the Gulf War. And during World War II, once the United States entered the war and victory was in sight, the Dow doubled between 1942 and 1946. Victory against dictators and those who would impose their "one and only truth" on everyone, brought about expectations of wealth.

Countries such as Canada, Mexico, Japan and those of Western Europe who have been languishing in bureaucratic stupor or worse during the last few decades, will be less able to count on the U.S. engine to pull them out and cover for their domestic political blunders. Because of the U.S. focus on both military and domestic affairs, these countries will have to restart their engines on their own and bring about changes to strengthen their own capital

the option of accessing developed capital markets in the first place.

Not surprisingly, Soviets not only turned back to the government, but also turned to crime (i.e., the violation of laws). Committing criminal acts to raise money is no more a zero-sum game after Communism than it had been during. Back then, black markets thrived, and without them Communism would not have survived even the seventy years it did. Today crime is a means of getting around Russia's devastating levels of taxation and tariffs, and its closed financial markets. Indeed, many of the so-called criminals are the entrepreneurial Robin Hoods of our time. And even if all citizens paid the onerous taxes instead of smuggling money out of the country, that would not make ordinary Russians any more prosperous.

Some say that what is needed in Russia today is a large grant from the International Monetary Fund (IMF). In truth, this money would simply subsidize the central government and prevent the drastic change that is needed to put Russia on the road to long-lasting stability. The grant was lobbied for under the mistaken belief that unless the center is subsidized, Russia will be destabilized, with grave political consequences for the United States and Western Europe. In fact, just the opposite is true: such subsidization gives the central government more power, which in turn sustains corruption and delays the democratization of capital markets. Moreover, the IMF's policies have succeeded in discrediting the notion of entrepreneurial capitalism and the role of the U.S.

Contrary to the conventional wisdom of today, a move toward democracy (free elections), when not coordinated with the democratization of capital markets, does not bring about prosperity. In the absence of collateral and open financial markets, government remains the main source of capital. Such conditions create pressures on governments to tax, borrow, and spend.

And ordinary citizens, with no access to financial markets, cannot borrow against future incomes. Thus promises of institutions to protect property rights stay abstractions. As paradoxical as it may sound, giving people the right to vote without giving them access to open capital markets slows down the process of estab-

to leave for the West or Israel. Israel's emergence on the commercial-high-tech map, becoming within ten years the country with the third largest number of companies listed on NASDAQ (following the U.S. and Canada), is due to the influx of a few hundred thousand highly trained Russian immigrants, and the rapid deregulation of its financial markets.

The Shanghai-based Chinese, their property destroyed and confiscated, similarly rose from the ashes in Hong Kong. The Chinese thrown out of Malaysia flourished in Singapore. Loss of family and property—tragic as they are—do not condemn people to poverty. People are condemned to poverty when political powers keep capital markets closed, thus denying people access to borrow against futures they would like to bet on.

Consider Germany after World War II: much of its infrastructure was in shambles and millions of lives were lost. Still, West Germany revived rapidly and communist East Germany did not. Germany recovered not so much because of the Marshall Plan, generous as that plan was, but because Ludwig Erhard, Germany's finance minister, carried out a drastic currency reform and severe tax cuts; Germany saw the influx of millions of skilled immigrants from Poland, Czechoslovakia and East Germany.

Crises quickly bring people back to fundamentals. The United States recovered rapidly from the Cuban Missile Crisis, the Kennedy assassination, and the Gulf War. And during World War II, once the United States entered the war and victory was in sight, the Dow doubled between 1942 and 1946. Victory against dictators and those who would impose their "one and only truth" on everyone, brought about expectations of wealth.

Countries such as Canada, Mexico, Japan and those of Western Europe who have been languishing in bureaucratic stupor or worse during the last few decades, will be less able to count on the U.S. engine to pull them out and cover for their domestic political blunders. Because of the U.S. focus on both military and domestic affairs, these countries will have to restart their engines on their own and bring about changes to strengthen their own capital markets. We can expect countries such as China and Russia to move in similar directions. The shift toward greater accountability will strengthen the West—and all countries that are in the process of democratizing their financial markets—both politically and economically. And markets will reflect expectations of the increased wealth creation.

In a recent lecture, Sir Michael Howard remarked: "people, often of masterful intelligence, trained usually in law or economics or perhaps political science . . . have led their governments into disastrous miscalculations because they have no awareness whatever of the historical background—the cultural universe of the foreign societies with which they have to deal. It is an awareness for which no amount of strategic or economic analysis, no techniques of crisis management or conflict resolution can provide a substitute." What Sir Michael neglects is that one gets far richer insights by combining such knowledge of the past with knowledge of the future. And that knowledge comes from one source: financial markets.

This book examines not only the U.S., but places as diverse as Russia and Africa; Mexico, Venezuela and Asia. The key to their prosperity would be to establish a system of checks and balances, together with rapidly democratizing financial markets. Since for the moment, the U.S. alone got these fundamentals right, the book shows why the twenty-first century will be another "American Century."

Reuven Brenner
November 2001

INTRODUCTION

In the past 225 years, a number of books have examined why and how nations prosper or fall behind. These include *The Wealth of Nations* (Adam Smith, 1776), *The Work of Nations* (Robert Reich, 1991), *The Wealth and Poverty of Nations* (David Landes, 1998), and *The Rise and Fall of the Great Powers* (Paul Kennedy, 1987). The last decade of the 1900s also saw the publication of several books on this same theme — *The Borderless World* (Kenichi Ohmae, 1991), *The Twilight of Sovereignty* (Walter Wriston, 1992), *Tribes* (Joel Kotkin, 1993), and my own *Labyrinths of Prosperity* (1994)— but now authors seemed to be looking beyond their own borders.

There are good reasons for going beyond national units when addressing these issues. It is true, certainly, that the United States has done better economically of late than many other countries around the world. It is also true that the Western democracies prospered far more than most other countries between the end of the Second World War and the late 1980s. However, within even the prosperous United States, pockets of poverty persist. Harlem and the Bronx are only a few minutes away from Manhattan's glittering Fifth and Park avenues. Virginia has its horse farms and rolling estates, as well as areas that are mired in poverty. And the United States is by no means unique in this. Canada includes the prosperous cities of Toronto and Calgary, as well as the functionally illiterate, poor province of Newfoundland. Italy is prosperous in the north, but its southern regions constitute little more than an emerging economy. A north-south division is now appearing in Mexico too.

Yet national statistics gloss over such realities. They also ignore the fact that, in many countries, sudden economic success has less to do with the entrepreneurialism of the local population than it does with the political blunders of other nations. These blunders lead to the rapid outflow of both capital and talented people. The people take their knowledge, skills, networks, and resources to new places, which thrive as a result. Hong Kong, Israel, and the United States are all countries where such a sequence of events brought about rapid prosperity. The countries the migrants left, meanwhile, fell behind.

This, then, raises questions—which this book attempts to answer—about the nature of prosperity, and about how poorer countries can catch, and even surpass, richer ones. Contrary to popular belief, democracy—that is, giving the people the right to vote—does not bring about prosperity. Mexicans have had the right to vote for seven decades (as have people in several other Latin American countries), yet Mexico remains a poor country. Meanwhile, people in Hong Kong had no right to vote, and yet that city has prospered.

If democracy doesn't bring prosperity, you may well ask, does access to natural resources? Again, the answer is no. Although the high prices such resources command bring riches, these tend to benefit those in power rather than the population at large. Mexico,

Argentina, Brazil, Venezuela, Zaire, Romania, and, in a sense, even Canada fit this pattern. In spite of their abundant natural riches, these countries either stayed poor or fell behind. At the same time, crowded, resource-poor, and disaster-rich places such as Hong Kong, Singapore, South Korea, Taiwan, Japan, Israel, and even Ireland have thrived, often leapfrogging their resource-rich cousins.

How?

To prosper, people must have access to capital, and societies have five sources of capital. The first three are inheritance (natural resources), savings, and, most important, capital markets. If access to these three sources of capital is hindered, there are two others left: government and crime. In many countries, these last two are hard to distinguish.

Government, in this sense, is a particular type of financial institution. It obtains its revenues from taxes and borrowing. It then makes matches based on political calculations, and redistributes those revenues to constituents. Once a government gains control over natural resources, closes capital markets, and—as happened frequently during the final decades of the past century—wipes out the value of savings through inflation and devaluation, people have few options left. They can push for political changes, resort to crime, or move to more hospitable shores (where capital markets are more open). When we see those occasional votes in favor of big government, they are not necessarily a sign that the voters are leftists or Communists, or even that they have been educated in paternalistic cultures or want to escape from freedom into safer authoritarian rule. Rather, these voting trends indicate that for most people moving is not an option, and the government, flawed as it may be, remains the main means of accessing capital and ensuring at least a minimal standard of living.

Put simply, prosperity is the consequence of one thing and one only: matching talent with capital, and holding both sides accountable. In countries with open, democratized capital markets, such matches are made by a wide variety of financial institutions, each employing an assortment of screening devices and contractual agreements, and they and other institutions ensure accountability. When capital markets are closed, government employees make the matches. Even if these people were as highly skilled in making investment decisions as their private-market counterparts in other countries—which is not the case—the level of accountability is not the same. Bureaucrats and politicians do not personally go bankrupt if they make disastrous matches. Often, they are also not held accountable.

Of course, this is not to say that venture capital firms, banks, and other financial institutions never make mismatches when allocating capital. They do. But they cannot afford to make very many mistakes, and they do not have the luxury of correcting their mistakes slowly. Governments, on the other hand, can make many more and greater mistakes, and they can also fail to correct them. They can cover their mistakes by taxing, inflating, and debasing their currency. These methods of financing government spending—none of which is available to private financial institutions—allow mismatches made by governments to persist. It is these links between capital markets and democracy that I explore in chapters one and two.

As I've noted above, one option left open to people when capital markets in their own countries are closed is to move. A dozen years ago, few people had this option. Since the fall of Communism, more people do. Indeed, that is what, at its heart, the word "globalization" means: easier and faster movement of people, capital, and ideas. Chapter three shows how such movement has made some places rich very quickly. The chapter also shows why societies transform so slowly from relative immobility to mobility. The process of adjusting political institutions and discarding falsely imagined pasts does not happen overnight.

These first chapters also address another question: Why have so few societies succeeded in developing democratized, deep, and open capital markets? The answer is that such markets depend on a certain kind of trust—namely, the trust that the law will be applied equitably to all participants in the long term. A maze of complex institutions is required to generate and sustain this trust. If people expect their governments to be run by kleptocrats (i.e., thieves) who will use their powers to make arbitrary changes to the rules along the way, they will risk far less capital and do so at a higher price than they would if sufficient checks and balances existed. It is wrong to say that the establishment in countries that kept their capital markets closed needed Adam Smith, Milton Friedman, or Friedrich Hayek to explain the benefits of opening them. They understood this only too well. But they also knew that nothing disperses power more quickly than democratized capital markets—just as nothing threatens a company more than competitors with access to cheaper financing.

It's little wonder, then, that the elites in most countries kept their capital markets closed, justifying their actions with a wide variety of mythologies, economic and financial ones in particular. Chapter four examines such modern mythologies, including the macroeconomic one. It also shows how referendums and initiatives—often referred to collectively as "direct democracy"—have the means to discipline governments at all levels by separating the powers to tax and spend. Such institutions cannot guard against occasional mistakes. Nothing can. But by giving the public veto power over specific spending decisions, direct democracy can prevent mistaken policies from persisting for too long.

Chapter five examines several economic mythologies, and shows that the foundation for a stable global financial architecture lies in establishing a monetary standard, separating monetary policy from politics, and significantly limiting the powers of the International Monetary Fund (IMF). One of the "institutions" that any society needs if it wants to insure developed capital markets is sound money. Yet economists over the past few decades have espoused a wide variety of theories suggesting that societies benefit from debasing currencies through inflation and devaluation. Paul Krugman of the Massachusetts Institute of Technology (MIT) is the most recent proponent of the view that an eternal level of inflation of 2 to 4 percent a year is beneficial. Do not ask why. Even a yearly inflation rate of 2 percent doubles the price level in thirty-five years. Yet that is not the only bewildering idea that Krugman and other economists offer today, as this book will show.

Chapter five also shows that these harmful mythologies about the benefits of unsound money serve narrow interests. Monetary issues are not as complex as economists and central bankers would have us believe. The confusion is in fact a consequence of what people want money to be, and what governments want to do with it. Since the business of everyday living is often about complex contractual agreements, people need a stable unit of account. If the unit is not stable, the contractual agreements become more complex and more expensive. As a result, people move to other currencies, take out a variety of insurances against the expected volatility of their own currency, enter into shorter-term contracts, or delay investments altogether.

However, governments—and rulers since antiquity—have discovered that they can use money to raise taxes through seigniorage and inflation. By the time the costs of mistaken inflationary policies and devaluation accumulate, the politicians have reaped the benefits and are safely out of office. Nobody has ever been held accountable for pursuing inflationary policies and debasing currencies. And economists have helped such politicians by transforming political lies into "science," in part by including them in university curricula.

What, then, is the path to sound money? Chapter five compares several methods: currency boards, monetary rule, inflationary targets, and the gold standard. As different as these methods are, they have one thing in common: they separate monetary issues from politics. Ideally, this separation would significantly diminish a government's ability to impose the inflationary tax.

Sound money also attracts capital from countries that are being mismanaged, quickly revealing the legal, fiscal, and regulatory mistakes the politicians of those countries have been perpetrating. Politicians can no longer blame so-called currency speculators for the flight (something they do when currencies are floating). Still, it would be misleading to think that, following periods of mismanagement, governments alone will resist sound money. Banks also benefit from increased transaction costs when currencies are fluctuating. In addition, financial markets, having developed sophisticated derivatives, stand to lose if countries suddenly stabilize their currencies. And last but not least, the IMF would find itself without much to do if all countries committed to fixed exchange rates.

Chapter six examines the origins of another harmful myth—nationalism—from an unusual angle. As the first chapters show, prosperity is made possible by opening up financial markets and building up institutions to bring about greater trust between people. These changes bring about more specialization, which in turn leads to greater dependency among the now specialized people. But what happens when the number of people within all "tribes" suddenly grows? Generally, they trust each another less, and new institutions must be invented to restore trust. People then have to relink within each tribe around new ideas (or they have to develop international institutions that would bring about greater trust between the tribes).

In Europe, from the eighteenth century until very recently, mistrust reigned as the number of people within each tribe increased. Members of each tribe bet on ideas that would bring them greater independence—an aim that was pursued under newly articulated "nationalist" doctrines. Two world wars and numerous other smaller ones, however, showed that this was an expensive road to follow. Fostering trust among tribes is now viewed as the better alternative—a venture the European Community has embarked upon. In chapter six, I will explore how people become entangled in harmful myths, and how they can disentangle themselves again.

One common theme that runs through the first six chapters is that many failures appear to have the same cause: Once a doctrine gains currency, it becomes harder for people, and even whole societies, to distinguish between perception and reality. As Tom Stoppard put it in one of his plays, "Politics, justice, patriotism—they aren't even like coffee mugs. There is nothing real there separate from our perception of them." Politics, businesses, universities, and think-tanks intermingle, supporting each other in sustaining misperceptions and mistaken policies.

These six chapters also try to answer the following questions:

How can we correct such policies faster? How can we achieve greater accountability in government? Can this particular financial institution—government—emulate the workings of capital markets? And can we create institutions that will prevent mistakes from lasting as long as they do today? If so, what will these institutions be?

Mark Twain once observed that education is not as sudden as a massacre but is more deadly in the long run. To have that deadly impact, facts must be stated again and again—and in a clear language. You would have thought that this is what education does, but as chapters seven and eight show, this is not the case. Subsidies have transformed institutions of higher learning into institutions where the humanities and social sciences have been turned into the arts and sciences of political lies, and most of which today offer—at best—equal access to mediocrity. Chapter seven, which borrows its title ("Extracting Sunbeams Out of Cucumbers") from Jonathan Swift's *Gulliver's Travels,* shows how this happens. If we want to leave the myths of the twentieth century behind more quickly, we should significantly restructure these myth-creating and -perpetuating institutions and put education on a sounder footing. Chapter eight, "The Future of Higher Education," shows how this can be done today. The final chapter, "A Financial Twenty-first Century," puts the final pieces in the puzzle and provides a picture for the future.

With the exception of chapter seven, this book is drawn from background documents prepared for speeches I gave to large audiences around the world, and sometimes from the speeches themselves. Hence I do not use jargon in this book, no matter how technical the subject. Though I make occasional cross-references between chapters, each one stands on its own. Put together, however, they give a better idea of how I see the world "working"—or "not working"—depending on the state of the financial markets of various countries.

CHAPTER 1

ANOTHER AMERICAN CENTURY

Prosperity is the result of matching brains with capital and holding both sides accountable. In every society, there are only five sources of capital. The first three are:

- inheritance, which comes to individuals from parents (bankers furnished by nature) and to countries from nature (through natural resources);
- savings; and
- access to financial markets.

If, for one reason or another, access to these three sources of capital is hindered, there are only two sources left: government and crime. Government, when viewed from this angle, is a particular type of financial institution, one with monopoly powers, the demand for which varies depending on what happens to the other sources of capital. Governments not only borrow money, but also take it by compulsion (through taxes). They then redistribute that money under various names to a wide variety of constituents. A government's success in bringing about prosperity from taxes and borrowing, on the one side, and spending, on the other, depends on three things:

1. How much "float"—that is, monopoly rents—it extracts from its citizens.
2. How the float affects people's behavior.
3. How the government spends the money.

Right away, we can make two observations about the above. First, the amount of float a government succeeds in extracting depends on people's ability to move. And second, the uses to which the money is put depends on the checks and balances imposed on the government.

The reason the float—that is, the burden extracted from citizens—is sometimes involuntary is that people often cannot move freely from one country to another, nor can they stay and vote for "shifting fiscal borders" within the country. Only Switzerland gives this latter option to its citizens, allowing fiscal borders to move while people stay put (I'll discuss this in more detail in chapter four). Most people around the world are not given such control over their local politicians, and thus they either are stuck in their situation or have to move.

If none of the three private forms of capital is available, and if a government is not fulfilling its financial role properly, people will sometimes resort to crime. Though the word "crime" implies violation of laws, this activity is not necessarily a zero-sum game. When the institutions offering the other four sources of capital are severely flawed, those who venture into criminal activities may actually help society (and not become a burden on it).

We can conclude, then, that countries prosper when better matches are made between capital and talent. And the corollary is also true: they become poorer or fall behind when the two are mismatched, and the mismatches persist. It turns out that lasting mismatches generate not only poverty, but also long-lasting ideological confusions. Let's examine now how this view sheds light on a wide variety of recent events.

THE EXPERIENCE OF THE FORMER SOVIET UNION

Consider the situation of ordinary Soviets in 1987, immediately following the fall of Communism. Over the preceding seventy years, Communism had wiped out inheritance. When the system fell, hyperinflation erased whatever meager savings people had. Since Soviets had no right of ownership of either land or apartments, they had no collateral against which to borrow and trade. And because of the federation's closed financial markets, ordinary citizens could not borrow against future earnings. Thus the Soviet Union could not prosper. Those who wanted to access capital had only two remaining options, much as they had had under Communism:

1. Return to a reliance on government.
2. Turn to crime (black markets).

It was easy to predict in 1987 that the Soviet Union would not prosper, and that its citizens would continue to support the Communist politburo. They had little choice: the government remained the main source for funds, whether people needed those funds to make a living or to insure the health and well-being of their children. One could also predict that calls for "shock therapy," the radical freeing of prices and markets, would prove to be superficial and short lived. In a world where people have no collateral and no access to capital, there can be no meaningful competition. Without open capital markets, "privatization" is a word without meaning. So-called privatized companies become de facto monopolies when capital markets remain closed, largely because no one can access the capital needed to set up competing businesses. Ironically, when people are denied access to capital because there are no open financial markets, many will turn back to the government for help—the same government that denied them

11

the option of accessing developed capital markets in the first place.

Not surprisingly, Soviets not only turned back to the government, but also turned to crime (i.e., the violation of laws). Committing criminal acts to raise money is no more a zero-sum game after Communism than it had been during. Back then, black markets thrived, and without them Communism would not have survived even the seventy years it did. Today crime is a means of getting around Russia's devastating levels of taxation and tariffs, and its closed financial markets. Indeed, many of the so-called criminals are the entrepreneurial Robin Hoods of our time. And even if all citizens paid the onerous taxes instead of smuggling money out of the country, that would not make ordinary Russians any more prosperous.

Some say that what is needed in Russia today is a large grant from the International Monetary Fund (IMF). In truth, this money would simply subsidize the central government and prevent the drastic change that is needed to put Russia on the road to long-lasting stability. The grant was lobbied for under the mistaken belief that unless the center is subsidized, Russia will be destabilized, with grave political consequences for the United States and Western Europe. In fact, just the opposite is true: such subsidization gives the central government more power, which in turn sustains corruption and delays the democratization of capital markets. Moreover, the IMF's policies have succeeded in discrediting the notion of entrepreneurial capitalism and the role of the U.S.

Contrary to the conventional wisdom of today, a move toward democracy (free elections), when not coordinated with the democratization of capital markets, does not bring about prosperity. In the absence of collateral and open financial markets, government remains the main source of capital. Such conditions create pressures on governments to tax, borrow, and spend.

And ordinary citizens, with no access to financial markets, cannot borrow against future incomes. Thus promises of institutions to protect property rights stay abstractions. As paradoxical as it may sound, giving people the right to vote without giving them access to open capital markets slows down the process of establishing these institutions. The reason is simple: property rights have little practical meaning when one does not know how much tax will be imposed on that property.

Debates about whether Russia would benefit most from the "rule of law" imposed from above, from an investment in infrastructure, or from the pursuit of the aforementioned "shock therapy" were wrong-headed too. One better route to prosperity would be to open up financial markets from the bottom, offering citizens a stake in the system (such as the opportunity to own their own— lightly taxed—apartments or land, which would then serve as collateral against which they could borrow).

But if working from the bottom up is the key to establishing solid foundations for an entrepreneurial society, two questions arise: Since democratized financial markets diffuse power, why would any politician in power agree to move toward such a goal? And if democratized capital markets are such a good thing, why have so few societies developed them?

The answer to the second question is that these markets depend on a certain kind of trust—namely, that the law will be applied equitably to all participants over the long term. Why then, you may ask, have so few societies adopted the institutions that would insure the generation and maintenance of such trust? We tackle this fundamental question next.

HISTORICAL REMINDERS

Much has been written about the fall of Communism, and recently there have been renewed discussions about just what made the Western experience so different from the Soviet one. The claim that "history" made them different is meaningless. The real question is this: What exactly in their history made Russians (not unlike the citizens of some other nations) obedient for so long to rulers whose shortcomings were plainly evident to most Western eyes?

Harold Berman, the late legal historian, went back to the Gregorian Reformation and the investiture struggle of the eleventh century to find the answers. According to Berman, these events in the West sharply separated the Church from the secular world of politics and governance, freeing the clergy from the domination of lords, kings, and emperors. This separation, Berman writes, "gave rise to the formation of the first modern Western legal system, the 'new canon law' . . . of the Roman Catholic Church, and eventually to new secular legal systems as well—royal, urban, and others." For centuries, the Church was the only institution capable of resisting royal and feudal authority.

This feature—the long history of struggle, of rivalry between the highest political authorities and the Church—distinguishes the Western experience. Even when these two powers were not fighting one another, the idea of the legitimate co-existence of the two—rendering unto Caesar the things which are Caesar's, and unto God the things which are God's—was always in the background.

For a sharp contrast, let's consider Russia in the two centuries before the October Revolution of 1917. For those two hundred years, the Russian Orthodox Church was governed by principles introduced by Peter the Great in 1721 in the Ecclesiastical Regulation. According to this regulation, the Church ceased to be an institution independent of government, and its administration became a function of the State. Peter's explicit goal was to abolish any possibility of competitive power in the land. He achieved his goal.

State control over the Church had a devastating effect. Although Russians could still find solace in orthodox services and the sharing of suffering in a church community, the Church could not play the same roles in society as its Western counterparts. This powerless Church, which occupied itself only with private spiritual matters and would not stand up to the government on behalf of Judeo-Christian values, soon lost the allegiance of the Russian "vital few." Two centuries later, Vladimir Lenin merely tightened the screws: he established a puppet patriarchate, and this was controlled by the State rather than the Holy Synod (an institution he abolished). This new patriarchate never uttered a word of criticism against the regime. The novelist Alexander Solzhenitsyn was right when he

14

declared that Russia would have developed a more civil society over the past centuries had the Church not surrendered its independence.

Solzhenitsyn has also contrasted Russian and Polish history. The same issues that Western Europe struggled with between the eleventh and thirteenth centuries (when the Church never fully bent to the will of the State) were debated in Poland after the fall of Communism. Czeslaw Milosz, winner of the 1980 Nobel Prize in literature, notes that the "strength of Catholicism in Poland during the last decades was enhanced by the fact that it defended human rights and provided a spiritual home to all people, believers or not, who recognized that Marxism was a philosophical sham. In contrast to nearly all European countries, Poland's highest-caliber periodicals have been run by Catholics, and this circumstance in turn added to the prestige of religion." But now, he adds, the Polish no longer want the Church as a political party. Rather, they expect the Catholic primate, Jozef Cardinal Glemp, to initiate a true division of Church and State.

It is no accident that Russia and the Islamic countries, like any others dominated for a long time by one authority, have much in common. These countries have had large and corrupt bureaucracies. They share a long history of arbitrary authority; of confiscation of private property; of forcing people to buy goods at high prices but sell the products of their own labor cheaply; and, in general, of forestalling the market—all while maintaining powerful police forces and armies. They also share the custom of bribery, a lack of productivity, and a general attitude of fatalism—with occasional outbursts of revolutionary ardor.

If the excesses of the Islamic leaders seem somewhat less flagrant than those of their once-Communist counterparts, it may be because their behavior in office is constrained by the same Islamic laws to which their subjects must adhere, laws that they may neither change nor, in general, interpret. Leaders who violate these constraints may be disobeyed, but since Islam does not prescribe ways to challenge such violations, it is not surprising that the subjects have often reacted by force.

These historical reminders answer the broad question raised above: Why have so few societies developed that "trust," the reasonable expectation that laws will be equitably applied, without which capital markets cannot develop? These reminders also help us make sense of circumstances that seem strange to us, such as the esteem in which the military is held in various countries (Turkey and some Latin American nations, for example). Support for the military is not necessarily a sign that the people in these countries favor dictatorships. More likely, it is an indication that the military is viewed as the only alternative institution that will be able to extract rights that elected but corrupt governments have refused to give to their citizens, beautifully written constitutions notwithstanding.

In Poland, the Catholic Church—rather than the military—was the only alternative institution that held some power against the monopoly of the Communist Party. Recent events in China can also be interpreted from this angle: the power center resists the emergence of competing organizations because these could so rapidly become the alternative source of power. Consider the party's recent ferocious reaction to what seems like a voluntary, non-political association: the Falun Dafa. And that country's leaders have shrewdly kept members of the military in check by giving them access to a wide variety of enterprises, which in turn gives them a stake in the new, emerging order. Few things endanger a new regime more than an army of unemployed, desperate soldiers and a military elite losing power.

Can Western democracies speed the process of dispersing power in these authoritarian states? The answer is yes, though simply espousing democratic principles is not the solution. If democracy is initiated by fiat, as opposed to being the culmination of a process, it is counterproductive, and will bring about stagnation and poverty. If a country does not have effective competition in the political sphere—a process that implies the democratization of financial markets (without which there could be no effective political competition, since all financial power would be centralized)—democracy only means that the populace can vote. Holding elections without offering a real alternative is a recipe for stagnation.

16

Remember that Mexico, Venezuela, and Brazil—all practicing a form of democracy—stayed poor for decades. Mexico saw the same party rule for seventy-one years; Venezuelans have, for the past forty years, watched two parties alternate power with a cartel-type agreement between them. Democracy became a façade—and the countries stayed poor. At the same time, that great non-democracy, Hong Kong, grew rich. It did take shelter under the umbrella of the British legal system, of course, and establish open financial markets. Exceptions disprove rules.

We must also remember that several post-Communist societies, such as Poland, Hungary, and the Czech Republic, have done better than Russia and other Eastern European countries. How do we account for this? People in the first three nations were isolated for only forty years, rather than seventy. They had better knowledge of alternative models of society, and, more important, their ruling parties allowed, even under Communism, competing institutions around which citizens could organize and extract some rights. Poland had the Roman Catholic Church and the Solidarity movement, for example, while Czechoslovakia had a tradition of radical student movements and dissidents. Hungary, for its part, had the inspiration of its 1956 uprising, which brought an end to the rigid Communism of earlier decades. Also, in all these countries, people already had some private property when Communism collapsed. And each had a diaspora in the West, members of which returned following the fall of Communism, bringing with them both human and financial capital, as well as highly valued networks (which I will discuss in more detail in chapter three).

But let's continue for the moment with some broader issues. The conventional wisdom is that democracies tend not to engage in wars, and so the U.S. should encourage the dissemination of democracy around the world. This is a superficial statement. Since the Second World War, no countries with nuclear capability have clashed, either. Does that mean that the best policy to avoid war is to arm every country with nuclear weapons? Of course not. Several times, democracies—such as those in Western Europe between the two world wars—have lapsed into dictatorships, and from there into wars. What we really need to focus on is preventing a repeat performance. How can we avoid another Weimar?

This is where Francis Fukuyama and Samuel Huntington both trip up. It is not true that we are at the "end of history," or that clashes between civilizations are inevitable. Without question, societies have lapsed from prosperity, rule of law, and democracy into dictatorships (when their capital markets are suddenly destroyed, as we'll see in the next section). And yes, some of these societies engaged in war. But this happens when nations find themselves not at the end of history but at tortured new beginnings. It is then that clashes between civilizations take place.

Still, democracy alone is not insurance against such a sequence of events. It must go hand in hand with the liberalization of financial markets, first by giving citizens a stake in the system. There is nothing that diffuses power more than opening financial markets, and there is nothing that helps centralize it more than destroying them. This destruction also brings in its wake long-lasting ideological confusions.

BETTING ON IDEOLOGIES

Let's go back to the 1920s and 1930s. We still live with the consequences of a past we falsely think existed then, and politicians and academics still imagine today's policy options in terms of the misleading vocabulary invented during that time. It was in the 1930s, too, that "capitalism" lost its glitter. Why?

What did people live through then? There was hyperinflation in Western Europe and massive unemployment in both Europe and the United States. Both led—as might have been predicted—to the drastic expansion of government powers. The resulting central planning went by various names—the New Deal in Franklin Roosevelt's U.S., militarization in Hitler's Germany. In the States, the Civilian Conservation Corps provided jobs in work camps for 3 million young, unmarried men, more than 10 percent of the country's workforce at the time. At first glance, this program would seem to share some basic features with Soviet-type central planning. Indeed, countries that previously relied on private financing adopted a variety of centralized approaches to their economies during these lean years, from "strategic" nationalization in Britain to government-business-labor corporatism in Germany and the New Deal in the United States.

Why? Well, in Germany, Austria, and Hungary, hyperinflation wiped out the savings of middle- and lower-class citizens and destroyed financial markets. And in the United States, 30 percent unemployment and 30 percent deflation led to a series of bank failures and bankruptcies, considerably weakening financial markets there.

In other words, our first three sources of capital, savings, inheritance, and financial markets, were destroyed in the Western world. Predictably, people turned to government and crime—crime organized by the State, in particular—and bet on new ideologies to justify the trends. People are very good at turning real issues to moral ones by covering them with a veil of language. Social scientists are eager collaborators in this, inventing new theories and vocabularies to legitimize regimes, be they racist, fascist, or Communist.

The word "crime" acquires a far broader meaning in such circumstances. There is an old clause in the laws of Ine of Wessex. If fewer than seven men attack private property, the law says, they are thieves; if between seven and thirty-five attack, they are a gang, and if more than thirty-five, they are a military expedition. If you multiply thirty-five by a few thousand, you will have the form German organized crime took in the 1930s. The situation in Germany was a reaction to the sudden eradication of people's wealth, owing to both hyperinflation and the burden imposed by the Treaty of Versailles. When they saw their wealth wiped out, and financial markets closed, some Germans turned to government and others to organized crime.

Economists in the 1930s failed to see that governments are asked to step in and act as financial intermediaries when financial markets are destroyed and people do not expect them to be restored. Instead of advocating the need to restore these markets, economists invented new languages to rationalize the centralist tendencies of the times. Governments then stepped into the financial void—becoming financial intermediaries of last resort—and used this new jargon to justify their actions. We still live today with the consequences of the fiscal, monetary, and regulatory policies invented then, and their misleading vocabularies. Those who draw on John Maynard Keynes's *General Theory of Employment, Interest and Money* are the best-known proponents.

Of course, this policy—having the government step in as financial intermediary—happened to be the right one in the 1930s, since most private sources of capital had been destroyed and economists had ceased to advocate their restoration. Instead, Keynes and his contemporaries gave the wrong reasons for the expansion of governmental power, suggesting, in a novel and most obscure language, that they had stumbled on some new "general theory" that could fit all times and make all societies prosperous.

Friedrich Hayek and Joseph Schumpeter, two economists who believed in business cycles and the invisible hand of the market, did not offer any solution during the 1930s. Financial markets held no place in their way of looking at the world. Instead, they just suggested waiting. Not surprisingly, this approach fell on deaf ears. People want to live first, and thus they will always bet on policies that restore hopes. In retrospect, it is strange that the "free market" and "business cycle" theorists of the time did not make explicit either the role of financial markets or the consequences of fiscal, regulatory, and monetary mistakes.

The proverbial forty years later (Moses and the biblical writers were on to something: that is how long we must wander in the desert to forget our period of slavery to another ideology and way of life), in the 1970s, several Western economies, including that of the U.K., were in trouble. They had by then been adhering for a generation to the Keynesian framework of fighting inflation with fiscal policy and recessions with monetary policy—a logic so perverse that only academics and politicians could have bought into it for that long. The experiment ended up with marginal income tax rates at 98 percent in the U.K. (at such levels, there is no real distinction between Communism and capitalism). Margaret Thatcher then rediscovered Hayek's views and the language of entrepreneurial capitalism, and framed her policies in those terms. One cornerstone was to turn a majority of Englishmen into property-owners— owners of their own residences, in particular—thus giving them a stake in the system and a benchmark against which they could evaluate government policies. In the U.S. in the 1980s, Ronald Reagan ushered in a similar policy shift.

This historical reminder offers lessons. Today, as in the 1930s, grave political, fiscal, and monetary mistakes have been the source of trouble around the world, the reason standards of living have slipped. In the political sphere, as in business, "necessity"—falling behind, that is—has been the mother of invention. People bet on new ideas during such times, or they at least reintroduce some old ideas into the public discourse. Adam Smith's were there for the picking for more than two hundred years, and Hayek's and Milton Friedman's for roughly fifty. But most countries had to fall way behind and get leapfrogged by others before they would bet on rediscovered ideas. Let us turn to more recent events to show—as Mark Twain observed—that though history does not repeat itself, it sure rhymes.

MEXICO AND VENEZUELA

After these historical detours, which have shown how some ideologies and new jargons come into being and others fall into disrepute, let us come back to the present to show how the "five sources of capital" theory sheds light on more recent events.

In the aftermath of Mexico's massive devaluation at the end of 1994 (a result of the secret printing of money by the country's central bank), many of its citizens, including those who had previously counted on prospering through legitimate means, turned to drug dealing. Though on the surface Mexico seems different from Russia, the magnifying glass of the five sources of capital soon reveals similarities that are striking. For the past seventy-one years, for example, elections in Mexico have meant practically the same thing that they meant in Communist Russia. In Mexico, until the year 2000, new presidents were selected by their predecessors, and all were members of the single ruling party, the Institutional Revolutionary Party (PRI). Legislators merely served whomever occupied the presidential chair. And never mind that on paper Mexican laws defined property rights. Most Mexicans, having no access to credit, were unable to acquire property. The judicial system was corrupt, and contracts were enforced not according to due process but by the payment of "dues" (bribes). Some 90 percent of the population lived in poverty decades ago, and the situation remains much the same today.

In Mexico, governments controlled access to credit, and the money went almost exclusively to the well-connected elite. It matters not how they got the money—through banks controlled by friends and colleagues, through taxes and subsidies, through credit extension with tariff protection, or through government ownership. The same people got the money for the same purposes, and that money was then spent in the same way. As a result, most would-be entrepreneurs have been left out in the cold, and the place continues to stagnate.

Such societies look "capitalist" from a distance, but this is a façade. We can use words such as "markets," "democracy," "rule of law," and "rights to property," as much as we please, but in reality these are cargo cults. The term "cargo cult" emerged on an isolated island in New Guinea. During the Second World War, airplanes would regularly arrive full of cargo, part of which was distributed to the natives. But after the war, the planes stopped coming. Distressed, the natives built thatched-roof hangars, a beacon tower made of bamboo, and an airplane made of sticks and leaves. Priests prayed for the cargoes to return. And waited.

Capitalism without open financial markets has turned many modern societies into cargo cults, and created much of the confusion permeating today's superficial discussions about "markets" and "capitalism." The forms and words seem familiar—constitutions, laws, banks, and courts are all there. And when "airplanes" arrive bearing treasures (in the form of high prices for natural resources, for example), the society even becomes richer. But the fundamentals— the ability to produce wealth consistently over the long term, rather than seizing on unsustainable quick fixes—are lacking, and the riches are quickly dissipated. This is why resource-rich countries—such as Venezuela, Argentina, Mexico, Brazil, Nigeria, Zaire, and various countries in the Middle East—all seemed to prosper for a while (as measured by misleading aggregate statistics), only to fall behind as soon as resource prices dropped. No political or financial checks and balances ever came into being in these countries. They may have adopted "capitalism" on paper, but they maintained their corrupt political systems and their closed financial markets in reality.

Let us wrap up this part of the discussion by reviewing other recent events. Observers are worried about how Venezuela's new president, Hugo Chavez, is concentrating power and changing the constitution. Yet Venezuela has been like Mexico. Behind the façade of democracy, the country has been riddled with special entitlements. There have been no strong institutions to provide checks and balances, two ruling parties have controlled power for the past forty years, and the middle class (and those aspiring to it) has fallen farther and farther behind.

Seventy percent of the population voted for Chavez in February 1999. But this does not mean that Venezuelans want big government, want to move to the left, prefer dictators to democracy. It simply means that when the judiciary is corrupt, when contracts are not enforced, when members of the elite collude to keep financial markets closed, people will turn to another source of power to try to extract rights. In most of these places, the only alternative organized institution happens to be the army.

True, people hope for enlightened despots. At times, as in the Chavez case, these despots come to power through the political process; at other times, they come through the military directly. In the 1970s, for example, when the extreme right and left clashed in Turkey, the military ruled for two years. But eventually power was given back to the civilians. In fact, the Turkish military has followed each of its three coups (the last was in 1980) with a rapid return to civilian rule. Today, Turks rate the military as their most trusted institution. It's not clear whether Venezuela will move in the same direction. Chavez may turn out to be the wrong choice, but the fact that he's an outsider is understandable.

If the goal is to extract rights from an entrenched establishment, Adam Smith and "free market" theories will never do. Most rulers know these theories very well—that is why they want to prevent competition and keep capital markets closed. Private citizens may not be able to articulate these theories as easily, but they understand nevertheless that without a countervailing power, they will not prosper. So they are pragmatic, and try to use the institutions they have. People want to live first and philosophize later.

On the surface, some of Chavez's recent acts—such as changing the constitution and disregarding Congress and the national election commission—seem non-democratic. But that's confusing pieces of paper with substance. Of course, there is a danger that Chavez will turn out to be a new dictator. But when the army is the only institution with the power to extract rights from corrupt governments, people do not have much choice but to support it.

CULTURE, FINANCIAL MARKETS, AND AMBITION

What can people do when financial markets are closed? When they cannot borrow? When there are no installment payments? What can they do with the small amount of disposable income they have when they cannot borrow against future income?

Since people in such situations are fated to stay poor, they spend small amounts on simple entertainments: drinking, gambling, going to pubs, and occasionally dressing up for a fiesta. Meanwhile, they sustain their hopes for a better life for themselves or their children by adhering to religious beliefs. This is not evidence of Marx's argument that religion is the opium of the people, however. Religion becomes a deeply institutionalized part of the culture of the poor when capital markets stay closed.

What happens if capital markets suddenly become democratized, such as is the case in Hungary and Poland today? Well, the effect is comparable to that of a leveraged buyout (LBO). Leveraged buyouts are transactions that take companies private, usually by buying up equity and taking on debt, with large interest payments. Just as debt disciplines and motivates company managers, it changes people's spending habits. If you save a hundred dollars a month but cannot borrow against future income (no installment payments), you will be able to buy durables only after long delays. With a loan, you can buy them now and regularly pay the debt. This is an incentive to make more efforts, work harder, and also to spend less on, say, cockfights and pubs. Indeed, national differences that many observers have attributed to "culture" may actually be adaptations made in a society with closed capital markets.

I never bought the famous Weber thesis that Protestant ethics made the Netherlands and the U.S. prosper. What did the trick was that these two places were the first in the world where the poor had access to venture capital, which in turn attracted talented people from the rest of the world, rapidly building up critical masses of human capital. Access to capital disciplined these people. Religion (that is, the Protestant work ethic) rationalized the new patterns, not the other way around. As I discussed earlier, we need ideas, religious or otherwise, to make sense of our own changing behavior patterns.

Democratized financial markets change cultures, motivate citizens, and generate civil behavior and hope. Of course, there is a price to pay, and those people who are not sufficiently disciplined often end up bankrupt.

CURRENCY, TRUST, AND FINANCIAL MARKETS

Currency is a crucial part of the prosperity puzzle for a simple reason: without sound currency, there can be no developed financial markets. We saw above what happens when financial markets are either closed or destroyed. Society changes and culture changes—political culture in particular.

But sound money alone is no panacea. Money may be sound, but taxes and regulations can still keep financial markets closed. Capital will not flow to such places, and—under a monetary standard—any regulatory and fiscal mistakes become instantly visible. This is reason enough for rulers and politicians to oppose sound money, and to subsidize pliable intellectuals to come up with theories "proving" that sound money is not a good idea, and that governments must keep open the option of debasing currencies.

This is part of today's macroeconomic gibberish. It always struck me as strange that economists believe that governments that cannot price chickens, eggs, shoes, or milk will know how to price federal funds. Or that those who pronounce themselves in favor of property rights and enforcing contractual agreements suddenly forget all about them when it comes to discussing monetary issues, when they advocate inflation and devaluation.

The macroeconomic jargon used today obscures a simple truth: there is a need for the separation of powers, for one institution to decide on spending while another upholds the value of the money. The move to narrow the distance between the two functions—and that is what is meant by "coordination" of fiscal and monetary policies (which is a cornerstone of macroeconomics)—is one source of the present confusion in monetary matters, and this in turn leads to monetary mismanagement.

The fact that money is the government's non-interest-paying debt (and like any debt, creates a range of problems if not honored) has been forgotten. Even economists who have argued for respecting property rights see no contradiction between this principle and the recommendation for 2 to 3 percent inflation a year. One finds this thesis in Paul Krugman's books, for example, particularly his latest, *The Return of Depression Economics* (which I'll dissect in chapter five). Many economists seem to have forgotten the fact that the vocabulary of financial markets is linked to trust (the word "credit," for example, comes from the Latin *credere,* which means to believe), and that no security can be created if there is no trust between the parties. It's no accident that bonds are called just that. They are supposed to bond—that is, be honored.

Let's look at the economic debates of the past few decades. Keynesian-type monetary policy has been confronted with policies based on one of four alternatives: monetary rule, currency boards, the gold standard, or inflationary targets. As different as these four alternatives are, they have one thing in common: they separate politics from monetary policy. Economists who have recommended any one of these options did so in an effort to restore trust in a currency so it could once again serve as a basis for contractual agreements and set the conditions for developing financial markets. (Chapter five examines the monetary and exchange-rate landscape in greater detail.)

We can now see that capitalism and ethics are not contradictory; trust is the very basis of both. With diminished trust, currencies are weakened. And with weakened currencies, capital markets are less developed, there is less prosperity, and the culture of the place (especially the political culture) changes too.

Let us now close the circle in this chapter by returning to the subject of matching talent with capital when financial markets are open. This will help us see why the U.S. has long been the "land of opportunity," and will continue to be so for the foreseeable future.

THE LAND OF OPPORTUNITY

The United States has created a society in which anyone with talent, energy, and the ability to organize has access to financial resources. Banks, venture capitalists, underwriters, and asset-management firms do not much care who your grandfather was or whether you dropped out of college. They only want to know if they can make money by backing you.

Such "democratized" capital markets are foreign not only to all of the countries examined above, but also to Japan, Germany, and

France. The economies of those countries are dominated by a few banks, with hardly any venture capital or LBO-type firms to speak of, and by corporations, with hardly any turnover on top. The combined value of public companies in Japan, Hong Kong, France, Germany, Italy, the Netherlands, Spain, and Switzerland is around $10 trillion. In the U.S., it's approximately $18 trillion.

The entrepreneurial, creative spark is probably randomly distributed around the world. However, the opportunities for that spark to burst into flame are not so evenly distributed. Opportunities for success in the U.S. are available to both foreign- and native-born entrepreneurs. This explains why so many immigrants come to the U.S., and why there are twenty-two foreign-born Americans on the *Forbes* 400, including John Kluge, George Soros, Fayez Sarofim, Jerry Yang, Bernard Ebbers, and David Sun, to just name a few. Together, these entrepreneurs—whom Jonathan Hughes, the late historian, called the "vital few"—in one generation accumulated net assets of approximately $40 billion. There is no other country in the world where immigrants can make such strides.

Just as cheap farmland once attracted the hardiest and most ambitious of Europe's poor peasants to America, so entrepreneurial opportunities now attract many of the best minds from around the world. These new immigrants do what similar people have done since time immemorial: move to places where political and family contacts matter less, and brains and ambition count for more. The newer the industry, the more the newcomers will have an advantage over the natives.

The U.S. does not have a monopoly on creativity, of course. Russian citizens are also innovative, and their abilities really began to show when some eight-hundred thousand moved to Israel. Forced to absorb them quickly, Israel deregulated its financial markets. Within a few years, the country had its Silicon Wadi (the Hebrew-Arab word for "valley"), and this was largely supported by the technical know-how of those Russian immigrants.

People have always been creative, but they have not always been given the opportunity and the incentives to bring their ideas to commercial life. That is where societies have differed significantly. Economists make much of their recent discovery that technological innovations are important to growth, with one economist, Paul Romer, particularly prominent in this field of study. Eh? What do economists think investors and venture capitalists have been doing for centuries? Anyway, it is the financing of technical know-how that matters, not know-how itself. The Chinese between the eleventh and fifteenth centuries had much of the technical know-how that brought about the Industrial Revolution in England in the nineteenth century. Yet the mandarins of the time ensured that China would not become a commercial society.

One unique advantage of the U.S. has been its open and sophisticated capital markets, which have made it possible for the smartest and most energetic of its citizens to exploit this know-how (another has been the "melting pot" idea, which I'll discuss in chapter six). No other country has the U.S.'s equivalent of junk bonds, securitized assets, angels, venture capital, initial public offerings (IPOs), LBOs, and the like. This openness has also attracted immigrants from countries that denied them access to capital. This inflow of human capital is not captured in the aggregate statistics that are religiously published by the government, but it greatly enriches the U.S.

Enriches by how much? Let us make a rough calculation. Taxed-to-death Canada suddenly noticed its brain drain in recent years. In 1997, about one-hundred thousand relatively young computer engineers, scientists, physicians, and other skilled professionals left for the U.S. Let's say that their average income is $100,000 a year. At a discount of 5 percent, the present value of that income amounts to $2 million. If we multiply the $2 million by the one-hundred thousand people who left, we get a transfer of $200 billion of wealth from Canada to the U.S. over a lifetime. No wonder the U.S. is prospering and Canada has been falling behind (contrary to silly United Nations polls that don't focus on personal incomes, and thus consistently rate Canada as the number-one country in the world).

There is nothing new in the rapid growth of some places and the equally rapid decline of others. When the Italian city-states of the Renaissance had open financial markets, they attracted the best people from the countryside. Amsterdam became the miracle of seventeenth-century Europe when it opened its financial markets, established the world's first stock market (where sophisticated derivatives were traded), and attracted people from around the world. Later, London became a financial and trading center by attracting craftsmen and financiers (from Amsterdam, among other cities).

Scotland, after its free-trade agreement with Britain in 1707, had the most open and democratized financial market ever. What had been one of the poorest provinces of Europe experienced an outburst of entrepreneurial energy, in this case with no immigration. Within a few decades, Edinburgh and Glasgow had become centers of trade and learning. The Scots became the great businessmen of the time, and Scottish Enlightenment thinking (which culminated in Adam Smith) was widely disseminated. The joke became that the Empire was conquered by the Irish, in the name of the English, for the benefit of the Scots.

The question is: If this is so simple, why haven't other countries done what the U.S. did and opened their financial markets as well? I have already given the answer, though it may sound discouragingly cynical to some: Making capital markets open to all diffuses power and threatens the privileges of ruling establishments. There is nothing that threatens any establishment more, in fact, than the act of allowing entrepreneurs access to credit. That is why, from ancient times, those in power have maintained a stranglehold on capital markets through a wide variety of regulations, rationalized by a wide variety of theories. Remember the usury laws? These laws made it illegal to charge people "high" interest rates. Though the laws were established in the name of helping the poor, they in fact had the opposite effect. The usury laws prevented people from having access to credit—even those with brilliant ideas and borrowers willing to back them. The dreams stayed dreams, the poor stayed poor—and the establishment stayed the unthreatened establishment.

Occasionally, even in the U.S., the establishment succeeds in imposing constraints on entrepreneurs, often disguising its blatant self-interest as an effort to protect the poor from the greedy. Most recently, we saw in the 1980s a concerted effort in the U.S. to crush the junk-bond market and put Michael Milken, the financial entrepreneur who turned this market into a liquid one, in jail. But what were junk bonds? In truth, they were little more than a financial instrument that would allow relative newcomers to raise money for the non-traditional ventures of the times, ventures that banks were unwilling to support. Think, for example, of CNN challenging the three networks, MCI challenging AT&T, Mirage wanting to turn Las Vegas into a more respectable place. These ideas were all perceived as outrageous at the time, and the great minds behind them all had to raise funds at high interest rates. The bonds, however, turned out to be anything but junk.

It is useful to look back and see how the business establishment and the old-line Wall Street houses tried to paint junk bonds as fraudulent or immoral. People are very good at turning real issues—such as their fear of competition—into moral or ethical ones. In this case, they succeeded in destroying Drexel Burnham Lambert, the junk-bond powerhouse, only to end up embracing that same business when the political storm had passed. This episode shows that the U.S. is not immune to mistaken policies and laws, and to rationalizing them with a veil of language. Still, the U.S. has not only more democratized financial markets, but also more checks and balances than any other country, and this allows such mistakes to be corrected more quickly.

The key to prosperity is to establish a system of checks and balances, together with democratized financial markets. That is why the twenty-first century, like the twentieth (apologies to Wilfrid Laurier), will belong to the United States. Of all countries—at least for the moment—the U.S. alone has the fundamentals right.

CHAPTER 2

CAPITAL MARKETS AND DEMOCRACY

Do elections necessarily have a substantial effect on public policy?

Is additional government spending necessarily inimical to prosperity?

The answer to both questions is no.

Consider, for example, several democracies in Latin America and Asia. Neither Mexico nor Thailand has moved toward "socialism," despite having given the right to vote to their respective populations decades ago. Most people in these countries were very poor when they got the right to vote—and they stayed poor. The right to vote did not lead to much income redistribution, either. Instead, something more important than voting rights—the openness of capital markets—had an effect on how much standards of living improved.

In other countries, too, the mere fact of being a democracy did not help predict the nature of adopted policies. In New Zealand, the United Kingdom, and the United States—all democracies—political leaders have, since the 1980s, reversed decades-long trends toward increased taxes, borrowing, and government spending. Starting with Margaret Thatcher's in the U.K. and Ronald Reagan's in the U.S., governments have changed their fiscal and regulatory policies to allow goods and services to be produced more often through private financing than through financing with governments serving as the intermediary. In the year 2000, even Canada's party in power woke up and moved slightly in the same direction, though without any real conviction.

We must recall, too, that although many democracies had already existed for decades, there were no significant movements toward redistributing wealth until the 1930s. Thus the evidence from both newly established and long-established democracies implies that something other than voting patterns has a dominant effect on what govern-ments do.

So the questions are as follows:

- Why are some decade-old democracies, which long ago extended the right to vote, not moving toward socialism at all, as many predicted they would?
- Why are 80 or 90 percent of the voting populations still poor half a century after their nations became democracies?
- Why do voters shift their demands—sometimes toward more government involvement, sometimes less?
- Why do governments in some democracies rectify their mistaken policies more quickly than those in others?
- What can explain these patterns?

This chapter will answer these questions by detecting regularities. It will show that the more widespread the checks and balances in a society—a situation that makes people more accountable in all spheres of life—the more quickly society rectifies its mistakes. Wonderfully written constitutions and rights to vote do not bring about prosperity. Open capital markets—even without democracy—do.

VOTES, POWER, AND CAPITAL MARKETS

In many Latin American countries, people held the right to vote but governments controlled capital markets. Frequently, just one party ruled, and a small number of well-connected families controlled that party. In Mexico, for example, as we saw in the previous chapter, elections have meant practically nothing for nearly seventy years. Legislators have merely served the occupant of the presidential chair.

This type of democracy may have had capitalism's form, but it didn't have its content. The vast majority of citizens—people who had no access to credit—were unable to acquire property. In addition, the top marginal income tax rate was standing at 35 percent. One reached the 32 percent tax bracket at US$4,000, which would have impeded the ability of poorer citizens to save and acquire property even if they had easier access to credit. The Mexican peso has not been a monetary standard; high inflation and each successive devaluation have cut deeper into the real incomes of the country's immobile citizens (that is, those who have failed to move—either legally or illegally—to the U.S.). Measuring high growth rates in terms of a currency depreciating at a still-faster rate indicates not prosperity but increased poverty. Take Canada as an example. Let's say the GDP, as measured in Canadian dollars, increases by 5 percent. If at the same time the Canadian dollar depreciates in relation to the American dollar by 10 percent, then, in terms of global purchasing power, Canada has become poorer by roughly 5 percent.

Faced with such "democracy" and such "capitalism," it's little wonder that Mexican capital, both human and financial, has moved—sometimes legally, sometimes not. The U.S. now has roughly 10 million citizens of Mexican origin (this does not include the estimated 2 to 3 million who are illegally in the country). After living for just one generation in the U.S., most are already—relatively—prosperous. But it's not just human capital that has moved

out of Mexico. During the December 1994 peso crisis, the first financial capital to flee was an estimated US$20 billion to $25 billion
owned by well-connected Mexicans. Economists have been on the
wrong track when attributing Mexico's and other countries' poverty
to "lack of savings." People in these countries did save. They just did
not want to put their savings to work in their own countries.

Latin American and Asian democracies are not the only ones
not thriving. Modern Turkey is another good example, as I mentioned in the previous chapter. Here is a country that is democratic
on paper, but that, since Kemal Atatürk's times, has been dominated by political parties that are tightly controlled by self-perpet-
uating elites. Much like inhabitants in parts of Latin America,
Turks consistently rate the military as the country's most trusted
institution. They credit it with preventing the country from lapsing
into chaos or falling under religious rule. As I noted in chapter one,
in a democracy such as Turkey's, such a role for the army is understandable. Its occasional intervention does not necessarily imply the
same thing that it does in a country with open capital markets.

What are we to conclude from all this? First, that extending
rights to vote while keeping capital markets closed leads to instability. Democracy has the effect of raising hopes. Keeping capital markets closed has the effect of preventing hopes from being realized.
Second, form and content in "democracy" and "capitalism" should
not be confused. Many countries have some of democracy's façade
but very little capitalist content. As a result, they do not prosper.
Keeping capital markets closed perpetuates an elite (since nobody
has access to credit to compete with it) and brings democracy itself
into disrepute. Unfortunately, as I will show next, this link between
capital markets, prosperity, and democracy escapes many observers.

DEMOCRACY AND PRIVATE OWNERSHIP

Here is what Arthur Schlesinger Jr., an influential historian, writes in a
recent piece in the journal *Foreign Affairs*: "Let us understand the relationship between capitalism and democracy. Democracy is impossi-

ble without private ownership because private property—resources be-yond the arbitrary reach of the state—provides the only secure basis for political opposition and intellectual freedom. . . . Democracy requires capitalism, but capitalism does not require democracy."

Schlesinger is right in stating that one cannot have democracy without private ownership. If all newspapers were owned by the state, or if the state controlled newspaper owners' access to credit, there would be no freedom of the press and probably little freedom of speech. Freedom of speech diminishes too as government spend-ing increases, because the government's advertising may become the media's main source of revenue. And to state the obvious, free-doms are diminished when governments control the airwaves or the production and importation of paper—a fact that did not go unnoticed by Romania's post-Ceausescu leaders. They adhered to free speech—on paper. But they insisted on controlling the alloca-tion of paper to the country's newspapers.

However, Schlesinger and others—his views are representative of large and influential schools of thought—are wrong. They emphasize the importance of the legal recognition of private prop-erty as a characteristic of democracy, but they never refer either to the state of their capital markets or to the existence of widespread checks and balances to ensure accountability in government.

Laws define property. But just as a farm cannot survive without water, so no business can start or expand without capital. One can own the farm, but the farm's value depends on the owner's access to water. If the government controls access to credit, the funds will go to the groups in control of government policies—and no one else. It matters only marginally whether the credit is re-allocated through banks controlled by an elite, whether it flows through taxes and borrowing and then is redistributed through government spending, or whether the credit is extended because of tariff pro-tection. The same people, for the same purposes, get the money, and it is spent in the same way. Thus "strategic companies" get healthy protection while powerless would-be entrepreneurs—as well as most citizens—get either nothing or higher prices.

The right to private property may be defined. But what if one can never get credit to acquire that property and accumulate wealth? What if the elite controls the banks and governments—the main sources of credit in these countries?

Historians', political scientists', and economists' complete disregard for and misunderstanding of financial markets when discussing capitalism and democracy is perhaps best reflected in another statement in the *Foreign Affairs* article. Schlesinger writes that "the capitalist market is no guarantee of democracy, as Deng Xiaoping, Lee Kuan Yew, Pinochet, and Franco, not to mention Hitler and Mussolini, have amply demonstrated."

I doubt if any serious observer would have called the countries under these dictators capitalist. The greater the role of the State in controlling access to credit, the fewer chances the poorly connected have to gain access to capital markets—regardless of whether "private property" is defined and the façade of capitalist institutions is maintained. Schlesinger falls into that "cargo cult" mistake discussed in chapter one, confusing form and content. Moreover, he seems to have forgotten what happened to the property of the Jews under Hitler and Mussolini. How is it that the influential *Foreign Affairs* publishes such superficial observations?

I am inclined to call on Alexis de Tocqueville for an answer. He wrote, in *Democracy in America,* that "in matters of language, democracies prefer obscurity to hard work. . . . Democratic citizens, then, will often have vacillating thoughts, and so language must be loose enough to leave them play. As they never know whether what they say today will fit the facts of tomorrow, they have a natural taste for abstract terms. An abstract word is like a box with a false bottom; you may put in it what ideas you please and take them out again unobserved." Schlesinger's text is a perfect reflection of this forecast. Chapters seven and eight will show how academia helps to establish this false language.

A place Schlesinger might have used to illustrate how "capitalism" works without democracy was Hong Kong, even before China's takeover. Of course, Hong Kong would have defeated his thesis and purpose, for this prosperous city reflects the reality that capitalism—meaning open capital markets—can prosper, even if citizens do not vote.

Since establishing a currency board in the early 1970s, Hong Kong has also had a strong currency. And it has an approximation of a low, flat tax (with a maximum rate of 18 percent). As a result, it has long been a place where people were able to accumulate wealth quickly—the magic of lightly taxed compound interest. Also, unlike even the U.S., Hong Kong's top talent did not have to specialize in the fields of law, accounting, and finance to learn how to overcome complex rules and high taxes. Rather, these people did more constructive things. And because of the openness of capital markets, even those people who did not become rich could expect their children to prosper—thus diminishing pressures on the government to "do something" (extend its role as financial intermediary, tax more, and redistribute more).

But alas, Hong Kong is an exception, and one from which we cannot draw many lessons. Since Hong Kong has no natural resources—and thus gains no rents from the high prices such resources sometimes attract—there are fewer pressures on governments to redistribute wealth and alleviate poverty. If governments in such a place tried to redistribute wealth unduly, the skilled, the traders, and the financiers—the mobile talents—would disappear within a short period of time, leaving behind the relatively immobile and unskilled, who would then become poorer.

The economist Milton Friedman attributed Hong Kong's success, in part, to Sir John Cowperthwaite, who was the colony's financial secretary from 1961 to 1971. He kept lowering taxes, balancing budgets, and opening markets—not only financial ones, but those for human capital as well (immigrants, that is). He believed in the theory of positive non-intervention. By this, he meant that he avoided being pressured into doing things by people who claimed to better understand how to spend money than the public does. But let me emphasize that Sir John could withstand such pressures not so much because Hong Kong was not a democracy, but because in a city built on rocks near the water there cannot be much to redistribute. To prosper in such places, one must use one's brains for a living, be engaged in finance and trade, and rectify mistakes quickly. Since the better brains are mobile, you can't tax them too much. Thus one should not expect Hong Kong's example to be emulated in other places—particularly not in places endowed with natural treasures.

The conclusion is simple: some countries have democracy's forms but very little of capitalism's content—meaning open capital markets—and these countries have not prospered. But the lack of prosperity had nothing to do with the consequences of extending voting rights to a poor population that then votes for high taxes and a variety of redistributive policies. It was not redistributive policies that kept these countries poor. Poverty was the consequence of an elite that perpetuated itself by keeping capital markets closed.

And the contrary is also true: Hong Kong prospered not because it did not extend the right to vote to the city's population, but because it kept its capital markets open, something it did in part because it happened to be a city that could not count on rents from natural resources.

One can reach an additional conclusion: the more often capital markets are open, the easier it is for people to find financial backing and succeed in their entrepreneurial ventures. As new people obtain financial leverage, they form new alliances, force debates, and reshape political coalitions, preventing anyone who reaches the top of the wealth pyramids from sitting on his laurels for too long. Opening up capital markets disperses power, and thus brings about de facto (but not necessarily de jure) democracy. The opposite process, as we saw, does not happen.

DEFAULT: A MOTHER OF POLITICAL INVENTION

Alexander Fraser Tytler (1748–1813) has been frequently quoted as saying, "A democracy cannot exist as a permanent form of government. It can only exist until the voters discover that they can vote themselves money from the Public Treasury. From that moment on, the majority always votes for the candidate promising the most benefits from the Public Treasury, with the result that a democracy always collapses over loose fiscal policy, always followed by dictatorship."

Tytler is wrong. There is a self-correcting mechanism: governments, whether democratically elected or not, change their policies when they exhaust their ability to tax and no longer have access to credit. The difference between a country with open capital markets and one with closed markets is that in the former, policies are corrected faster.

The economist Joseph Schumpeter was among those who noticed that whenever rulers' or governments' coffers were empty, political institutions crumbled and new ones replaced them. When governments do not have access to credit and cannot increase their revenues by taxing more, they have to cut their spending and change institutions. Fear of default is frequently the mother of invention in business, and so it is in politics.

How does this happen?

Public debt is backed by a government's right and ability to tax. It is backed by expectations that a country's citizens can create sufficient wealth, which the government can then tax. The expected tax base depends on a government's fiscal, regulatory, monetary, and immigration policies. When policies are such that creditors expect default—*and* no bailouts by the IMF—the government is unable to pursue its spend, tax, and borrow policies.

Here are some historical reminders of drastic political changes that happened when governments no longer had access to credit. The English war effort in 1666 against the Dutch was hindered by a lack of funds. But after the Glorious Revolution, the English did not find it difficult to raise money. A century later, French commentators correctly identified the origins of this British financial success as the move from an absolutist to a constitutional monarchy, which separated powers to tax from powers to spend.

The French were preoccupied with this question because, by that time, their monarchy was no longer able to secure new loans. The French Revolution followed. In his 1876 *Origins of Modern*

41

France, Hippolyte Taine, the great French historian, wrote the following about how France had arrived at such a state of financial affairs: "The state became the universal debtor; from then on, public affairs were no longer solely the King's affairs. His creditors became concerned about his expenditure, for it was their money he was wasting; if he mismanaged things, they would be ruined. They desired to know his budget in detail, to check the books. . . . Here then we see the bourgeois raising their heads and beginning to look more closely at that great machine whose working . . . had until then been a state secret. They became political animals and by the same token discontented."

I would ask (parenthetically): If creditors then could play these roles against the king of France, why can't private banks play this role today? Why does one need an unaccountable IMF staff to play the role, particularly when the IMF's bailouts to corrupt governments have had the effect of prolonging the rule of today's "kings" and kleptocrats?

Consider more recent examples of defaults that led to drastic political changes. After the end of the American Revolution in 1783, the finances of the new nation became chaotic as the government authorized expenditures without first establishing the power to tax. The financial and political system broke down in 1786, when, in spite of the new country's potential, the government could not secure loans—either abroad or at home. The prospect of default led to the Constitutional Convention of 1787. Likewise, the Meiji Revolution in the 1860s in Japan came about when the old Tokugawa tax system crumbled and the treasury was empty.

The fall of the U.S.S.R. fits into this well-known, long-identified pattern too. By the late 1980s, Soviet coffers were empty—Ronald Reagan's Star Wars initiative helped speed up the bankruptcy—and the government could no longer either tax its citizens or borrow—at least not so long as investors expected Communism to persist. I know there are many interpretations of Communism's fall. I do not find the others convincing. Regardless of the information the Soviet people had about better living conditions elsewhere, there was not much they could do as long the government had the funds to maintain a powerful police force and army to keep people fearful and obedient. Bankruptcy makes an establishment collapse—and collapse suddenly—be it in business or in politics. One difference between businesses and governments is that the latter can persist longer in accumulating mistakes than businesses because of their ability to tax (the occasional unexpected inflations are just a particular form of tax).

Why could Communism exact more suffering—through taxes and otherwise—during the 1930s than it did during the late 1980s? Why can countries pursue mistaken policies for so long? There are a number of answers to these questions. First, political alternatives around the world did not look very promising during the 1930s. There was in the U.S. the Great Depression, with its 30 percent unemployment; high unemployment also dogged Western Europe, where people were living with the consequences of the hyperinflation of the 1920s.

In addition, the devastating costs of Communism had just started to pile up. It was only in 1927 that Joseph Stalin came to power and abolished Lenin's New Economic Plan (NEP), which was a move away from Communism, in that it gave rights to peasants to hold land and own small businesses. Mistaken political experiments in one society can persist—especially when other societies make mistaken experiments of their own.

But some societies correct their mistakes more quickly than others. Capital markets eventually constrain the ability of governments to accumulate mistaken policies, if only because they make such mistakes more visible. They are the ones that prevent Tytler's conclusion that "democracies cannot exist as a permanent form of government." On the contrary, combining democracy with open capital markets is the best insurance against persisting with mistaken policies for too long.

Here is how the combination works. In its September 28, 1994, issue, *Strategic Investment* writes the following about Western democracies: "Government expenditure may have brushed up against its limit. Government bond auctions in Germany and Austria have recently been canceled due to lack of demand. . . . Could global bond markets be telling us that the Western socialist Welfare State has hit the brick wall of market limits on government debt issuance?" The article further remarks that as government spending and deficits in both Sweden and Finland have swelled over the years, investors have dumped Swedish and Finnish bonds. In 1994, although all Western European government bond markets fared badly, yields on Swedish and Finnish government debt rose especially sharply. In February of that year, the difference in yields between ten-year German government bonds and Swedish and Finnish ones was slightly more than one percent. By November, the difference was more than 3 percent. In 1995, Sweden had to cancel bond issues due to lack of demand. Investors had begun to worry about default—though one that was not expected to take the form of a cessation in interest payments.

A halt in interest payments is just one of the ways a default on a government's obligations occurs. Inflation and devaluation are other ways, even if legally they are not called defaults. The fact that the price of Finnish and Swedish bonds denominated in foreign currency did not fall as much as that of those denominated in the respective local currencies meant that investors were discarding the option of an interest payment default, and expected inflation and devaluation instead. By demanding higher returns to hold these countries' government bonds, investors signaled that they wanted higher compensation to offset the expected costs of possible defaults brought about by inflation and devaluation.

It is at this stage that one can see why Tytler's conclusion is erroneous. A democracy's widespread system of checks and balances makes for more extensive debates and consultations, dissecting signals from financial markets in particular. These debates allow for a more consistent and predictable process of detecting the causes of mistaken government policies. The public debates also enhance the credibility of the resulting political changes and reforms. In societies where such debates do not take place, the transition will be slower, with the persistence of mistaken policies bringing about increased misery.

Although it may be true that occasionally the "right person" at the "right time" in the "right place" can both prevent mistakes and correct them more quickly, such a situation is accidental, unstable, and cannot be relied upon. Democracy was expected to be a solution for exactly this problem: replacing the wisdom of one man with the wisdom of many, thus creating smoother political successions.

However, for real debates and peaceful political succession to take place, capital markets must be open. The more open they are, the more meaningful the debate and the smoother the transitions, since open capital markets, more than anything else, disperse power.

Campaign Financing: A Comment

What does all this imply for ongoing debates about campaign financing in the United States? What effect can methods of financing have on the persistence of mistaken policies?

One reason mistaken policies are corrected more quickly in the U.S. than even in, say, the U.K., France, or Canada is that political candidates in the U.S. do not have to adhere to the strict party line—Democrat or Republican. Once elected, they vote independently. Making politicians accountable to voters, rather than forcing them to follow the party line, serves as an additional check to prevent mistakes from lasting too long. But even this arrangement could be circumvented if the candidates were not able to rely on competing financial sources, and instead had to rely on money channeled through their respective parties (as is the case with Canada). Yes, financing makes the world go round.

Instead of imposing restrictions on donations, which anyway can be circumvented in endless imaginative ways, it would be preferable to let anyone donate as much money as he or she wanted. The law should force disclosure of the source of financing, however, making it transparent. People will not be fooled—and the media and the opposition will not let them be fooled even if candidates try—by a vigorous defense of a policy if it's known that there is a link between money and the advocated policy. The electorate will be skeptical.

But one can ask: What if someone rich buys up all the candidates? First, he will buy up only those serving his interests. Second, once his intentions become known, there will be so many opportunistic candidates pretending to represent his interests that the potential financier of campaigns will soon become very poor.

Another reason to require transparency rather than limits on donations is that unfettered campaign finance allows the decentralization of influence. If there are limits on the amounts of money raised, someone in the candidate's office will make choices about who has access to him. The candidate still has only twenty-four hours a day, no matter how many donations he gets. Unless the law requires the choice to be made by lottery (with an impartial casino to enforce the drawing of lots), the limits on campaign financing are an invitation to bribery—and its possible incarnations are endless.

Thus, whatever the angle from which we approach the subject of democracy and prosperity, the finding is the same. A key to prosperity and true democracy—not one on paper, defined by extending voting rights, but one having competing groups with financial leverage—lies in opening up capital markets.

THE WEIGHT OF THE PAST

Let us approach this discussion about links between capital markets, democracy, and prosperity from another angle. Once people have the right to vote, is it true that voters' demands for government-financed activities—in addition to defense, law, police—are necessarily a mistake? The answer to this question is no, too, and it has nothing to do with ideology.

Every society inherits laws, regulations, and intricate institutions. Even if they're wrong-headed, these inherited institutions, decades and centuries after they came into being, still routinely affect voters. It is consequences that voters observe and live with, not "causes."

Historians, economists, politicians, and the media, among others, compete to free us from falsely imagined pasts, to explain how a society got to its present stage, and how it may conceivably get out of it. Politicians and the electorate buy in to one explanation or another, and in a democracy the voters cast the ballots. The question is, Why does this sometimes lead to demands for more government-mediated financing of certain activities and other times lead to less? Instead of initiating an abstract discussion, I'll give examples to make one category of voters' demands for government financing clear.

I'll start with a somewhat esoteric example, but one that nonetheless helps make my point, I hope. Suppose we had a referendum today on whether governments should continue to subsidize orchestras, ballets, and opera houses. My guess is that a majority would vote for continuing to do so not only in Italy, Germany, and Austria, but also in the United States.

Here is how I see government involvement in the financing of this particular segment of the entertainment business. Until about 200 years ago, impresarios owned the great opera houses in Italy—Naples' San Carlo and Milan's La Scala among them. They were not just privately run, but also profitable. They were sustained by casinos adjoining the theatres, where rouge-et-noir was the favorite game. Rossini, for example, got a meager two hundred ducats a month as the musical director of the San Carlo, but he earned another one thousand ducats from his share of the house's gambling tables. The opera-casino combinations were the entertainment complexes of their times (Monte Carlo is a modern-day reminder of the once customary arrangement), and their profits also paid for R&D—that is, the commissioning of new ballets and operas. Politics put an end to the business, however, when the casinos were outlawed.

From then on, opera houses were forced to depend on subsidies, and governments stepped in to prevent them from closing. Some ventures cannot stay commercially alive if denied the option of being offered jointly with other goods or services. Imagine what would happen to movie theaters today, for example, if U.S. health authorities banned the sale of popcorn and soft drinks (which account for about 40 percent of theater revenues) on the grounds that they are not healthy. In fact, movie theaters get about 80 percent of their margins from this junk food, and only about 5 percent from the sale of tickets. If the sale of the food was prohibited, most movie theaters in the U.S. would close.

Since people would not tolerate their closure, they would start lobbying their politicians. Thus unless the prohibition of soft drinks and popcorn was canceled, the stage would be set for socializing movie theaters (that is, financing them by taxing people and redistributing the money to the theater owners). Or perhaps people would vote for outright state ownership rather than subsidies. (With the prohibition of cigarette ads in Quebec for some events, for example, the car-racing business and the jazz festival are already looking for government sponsorship.) True, those in the government department responsible for financing and managing movie theaters would be less adept than private entrepreneurs, because the administration would be more complex, politics about locations and standards would get in the way, and so forth. But at least the voters could go to the movies.

So let us return from this example to the case of a referendum on continuing subsidies to opera houses. Here we have voters today having to deal with an issue as much as two hundred years after the current arrangements came into being. No entrepreneur will be able to come forward and show voters that he can obtain financing to keep his opera house open if the government withdraws the subsidies. How will people vote? They will vote for continued government financing of this cultural institution.

Cultural experiments are hindered not only because of this prohibition, but also because of high capital gains taxes. After all, every new movie, ballet, musical, or opera is an R&D project, even if not called that. There may be ten thousand movie scripts written a year, one thousand read, one hundred translated to film, and twenty made profitable. Unless taxes are kept low enough to allow investors to expect high returns from the profitable twenty—so as to cover both the losses on the eighty failures and the costs of keeping in business those who filter down the selection to one hundred—cultural experiments will not be privately financed. In countries where capital gains taxes are high, the voters observe the decline in cultural enterprises, do not make the link with capital gains taxes, and vote for their governments to subsidize "culture." True, the votes lead to a distant second-best outcome—although lowering capital gains taxes would be the better alternative. But that option and the link between taxes and culture are, for the moment, out of most voters' field of vision.

The burden of either regulation from a distant, forgotten past or badly placed taxes prevents the financing of this particular business today. But most people want a vibrant culture, and they communicate this desire to their politicians. The electorate is not aware of the links between either gambling regulations and cultural ventures, or taxes and such ventures. While historians and economists carry on totally misleading debates about whether "culture" can exist in "free" markets, paying scant attention to facts and financial issues, the electorate wants to be assured that it gets the entertainment. *Now.* Politicians respond by promising to keep the cultural institutions open by subsidizing or nationalizing them.

What we observe today is that after some two hundred years, governments rediscovered gambling but kept for themselves the monopoly on the sale of lotteries—even though they had promised voters they would finance cultural establishments (and education) with the tax receipts. In an awkward way, the government became the financial intermediary, recombining casinos and culture under its own umbrella while denying the same option to the private sector.

Does government financing make the situation worse? As long as the prohibition on casinos stays in place, the answer is no. But casinos (and gambling in general) should be treated as a business like any other and should allow people to combine them with other lines of business. If this was to be done, governments' roles in financing "culture" could diminish.

We are already moving in that direction. Mirage Resorts CEO Steven Wynn has transformed Las Vegas over the past few years from a sleazy place to one offering family entertainment, including the Cirque du Soleil, Broadway musicals, and a gallery of high-quality Impressionist paintings. Luciano Pavarotti has been singing in Atlantic City's casinos. Maybe Donald Trump will take the next step and buy the rights to build a casino tower above New York City's opera house or Washington's Kennedy Center, and we'll be back to the arrangements that were interrupted two hundred years ago.

However, before people recombine these options, someone will have to come before the public, explain the long-forgotten commercial possibilities, and spark debate. Meanwhile, the weight of legislation regulating the gambling sector, which in most people's minds is not just unrelated to "high culture" but associated with its opposite, leads the electorate to vote for perpetuating the government's role as a financial intermediary in the entertainment industry.

One cannot say that the exercise of democracy in this case is inimical to prosperity. True, it is a second-best option. But if one wants to get to the best option, one must persuade voters what "the best" could be, and which regulation or tax prevents us from getting there. Until then, that "best" does not exist. What's out of sight is out of mind. And since people want to live first and philosophize later, they vote for financing cultural enterprises by governments.

Roads to the Future

Let me offer a less esoteric example to show the connection between mistaken policies and voters' subsequent demands for socializing activities and redistributing wealth.

Consider the following: In September 1995, fourteen-mile road in Virginia linked Dulles airport and the town of Leesburg. The Virginia road is privately owned—the first private toll road to be built in the U.S. in more than a century.

Whatever the origins of the U.S. government's decision to finance highways and bridges—some attribute it to the Cold War, to city dwellers wanting quick escape routes in case Russian atomic bombs hit—their present free use amounts to a large, implicit subsidy to carmakers, car owners, and those who fled cities for the manicured lawns of suburbia.

The subsidy diminishes significantly the advantages of commuting by trains and of using railways for the transportation of goods. The subsidy also significantly diminishes the railways' commercial value, and it has other costly consequences as well. It increases pollution, increases congestion, and empties the downtown of inhabitants, with all the attendant negative implications, not the least of which is the concentration of the less mobile poor in what become "inner cities" and the dispersion of a critical mass of talents from the city.

Whatever it was that led the U.S. government to get massively into financing the highways, once cars were thus being subsidized it became hard, or even impossible, to finance other means of transportation. The electorate (the same electorate that might have been persuaded that there are advantages in massively subsidizing highways), on observing the decline or disappearance of those alternative means of transportation, might vote for subsidizing railways, undergrounds, bus services, and air terminals.

Threatened by the increased crime rates in the inner cities, which are populated by the relatively unskilled and poor who stayed behind when the better skilled and higher paid fled to the suburbs, the electorate might also vote for spending more on police forces, urban-renewal projects, and the redistribution of wealth in the form of welfare programs. Threatened by the increased pollution, they also demand additional regulatory measures to deal with that problem.

These demands can be traced back, in part, to what, with the passage of time, people may learn was either a mistaken decision of the government's or an inevitable, inadvertent consequence of war. By the time the unintended, costly consequences of the government's financing of highways becomes evident, parts of the electorate—the car producers, suburbanites, enterprises that chose their locations based on subsidized-highway considerations—have adjusted to the subsidies. They would stand to lose significantly if, say, highways were suddenly privatized.

Thus a decades-old intervention has created powerful groups for its maintenance—even if the costs of its unintended consequences (such as inner-city poor) keep accumulating. At what moment do these costs exceed the benefits to the groups that benefit from the existing arrangements? Nobody knows.

Indirectly, a Canadian intervention sheds light on such costly unintended consequences. Before the Canadian government made the mistake about a generation ago to pay unemployment benefits to those engaged in seasonal work, Newfoundland's fishermen found employment during the off-season in logging, farming, weaving nets. New unemployment benefits, decided on in distant Ottawa, put an end to fishermen's incentives to look for and do these other jobs. They started to be paid not to look—with devastating long-term consequences.

Today, a generation later, Newfoundland has sixty thousand fishermen who are unemployed for most of the year, have forgotten all other skills, have lost both the intricate network of off-season employers and the credibility they once had within this network, and do not know any trade other than fishing. And that's a problem because, by now, there seem to be more fishermen than fish there. Iceland's six thousand fishermen fish more than Canada's sixty thousand—and the latter have six thousand fishing bureaucrats above them.

Imperceptibly, over a generation, the fishermen, who became dependent for their livelihood on government handouts, did not pass to the next generation the complex knowledge of people, activities, networks, and markets they once possessed. So what do you do with these people today? They have no marketable skills, no contacts, no credibility. Who will pay for their retraining? How do you rectify the consequences of a long-lasting government mistake? For now, Canada's fishermen fish in the place they were taught to fish: in Ottawa's ocean of spending.

As was the case with culture, one cannot say that if people vote for a government-financed program—for the poor and unskilled, in this case—the resulting government intervention will be inimical to prosperity. Something must be done with these people, after all. In other words, it is not the case that democracy inevitably brings about votes for interventions and redistribution. Rather, these votes may occasionally be symptoms of the electorate's wish to solve problems that are the unintended consequences of mistaken regulatory or fiscal decisions.

Mistakes and Responses in Financial Markets

As a final example of such a sequence of events—when voters ask for governments to play the role of financial intermediary not because of any solid conviction or self-interest—let's consider the bankruptcy of several saving and loans associations in the U.S. in the 1980s.

The problems of S&Ls started with Regulation Q, which prevented banks from paying interest above a certain limit. The S&Ls initially persuaded Congress to allow them to pay 0.75 percent more than the banks; this was reduced to 0.25 percent by the late 1970s. As inflation rates increased but Regulation Q stayed, however, people began withdrawing money from both banks and the S&Ls. Depositors put their money in mutual funds and CDs (certificates of deposit) for better returns. That left the S&Ls holding long-term mortgages at relatively low fixed rates. As well, their short-term deposits, which had financed these mortgages at rates as low as 5.5 percent, were evaporating, and the managers, to attract new funds, were having to offer interest rates above 10 percent. Technically, many S&Ls were bankrupt.

Finally, in 1981, Donald Regan, as the secretary of the Treasury, eliminated the interest rate restriction so that the S&Ls could pay depositors whatever was necessary to attract the funds they required. However, the S&Ls, having enjoyed decades of assured profitability because of the advantage the government had bestowed on them, were not able to assess the risks associated with giving loans in a competitive market. Still, their depositors had nothing to fear. While one regulation was eliminated, another— government-guaranteed deposit insurance—stayed. This allowed the S&Ls to assume far more risk than they should have, and it also made depositors complacent about doing their homework.

In other words, as long as deposit insurance was in place, additional regulations were needed to prevent these institutions from investing the money as they wished. When all regulations but deposit insurance were canceled, the S&L managers ventured into investment areas that they were incompetent to assess. The taxpayers were then stuck with the costs of the resulting bankruptcies. In general, once there is a mistaken intervention, an additional one might be needed to rectify the unanticipated effects of the first. That is how societies get into mazes of error and confusion.

But government interference with capital markets has a long history. One can go back to the McFadden Act of 1927, which barred national banks from carrying on their activities at any place other than authorized branches. The act was meant to put state and national banks on an equal footing, but instead had the effect of limiting interstate banking. This prevented banks from diversifying away from regional risks. Then the Glass-Stegall Act of 1933 (introduced by a mistaken theory of the Great Depression) separated commercial and investment banking. This prevented banks from diversifying their risks with other investments. Once the government makes risk-diversification impossible, the existence of federal deposit insurance forces it to get even more deeply involved to prevent the banking system from falling apart.

These brief reminders from financial history offer lessons similar to those drawn from the previous examples. First, a problem caused by government (providing deposit insurance) had to be solved by another regulation (limiting financial institutions' options to invest). Second, the U.S. would have been better off if there was no deposit insurance to start with, thus placing responsibility on customers and liability on producers.

Maybe in this case it was easy to identify the origin of the problem and abolish deposit insurance. But it is also possible that most voters did not link—and do not to this day —the S&L bankruptcies with old laws and partial deregulation. Greed, corruption, and bribes—not to mention sex—make for far better newspaper headlines than the effects of partial deregulation.

Consider now another complex example linked to financial issues.

How do voters react to the consequences of devaluation? Mobile talents, which are in demand in countries with stronger currencies (say, the U.S. dollar), will have the power to renegotiate their contracts following a devaluation. They will then sign them in terms of U.S. dollars. Since less-skilled employees are not as mobile, and financial capital is more mobile than labor, devaluation lowers the incomes of the less skilled. A similar process can be the result of inflation pushing people to higher tax brackets. The mobile talents have more power to renegotiate their contracts than the immobile ones, and thus can keep their after-tax income stable. (How many good hockey teams is Canada left with since its currency sunk to "dollaretto" status?)

Whether it's because of devaluation or a result of being pushed by inflation to higher tax brackets, the relatively immobile bear a disproportionate part of the burden of such mistaken policies. Among the unintended consequences of devaluation and inflation are further demands by voters for redistribution—by either peaceful or less-than-peaceful methods—bringing society into an ever deeper, costly maze of error.

But voters may not trace their diminishing standards of living to their government's erroneous monetary, exchange-rate, and fiscal policies. Let us not forget that until just a few years ago, most economists bought into Phillips curves, which suggested that central banks can plan to inflate, and by so doing the government could count on diminishing unemployment. And the IMF has been recommending devaluation with religious regularity.

Where can such a process lead? Just as capital gains taxes prevent the formation of capital, devaluation and high and progressive income taxes turn out to be taxes on human capital. As the futurist George Gilder once put it, taxes may redistribute not incomes, but taxpayers. A first sign that "income" taxes—in spite of their name—are being imposed on capital is that the top talent has started to move out of a country. By losing its pool of talent, and as a result failing to attract financial capital, a devaluating country can fall into a vicious downward cycle. It first loses human capital, then it fails to attract financial capital. This lowers further the wages of the relatively immobile and unskilled, which in turn increases their demands for redistribution. Then the cycle starts again, making society poorer. Sooner or later, the government's coffers are empty and the country's ability to borrow is diminished.

Accumulating Mistakes

In democracies, governments are frequently asked to fix problems past governments brought about, a process that often leads to additional mistaken decisions.

Each mistake is a cost, and costs accumulate at a compound rate. That's when the pendulum swings back—with capital markets playing a key role in the speed and force of such swings. In other words, it is not the case that democracy inevitably brings about votes for interventions and redistribution. Rather, these votes may be symptoms of the electorate's wish to solve new problems that are the unintended consequences of earlier mistaken regulatory or fiscal decisions.

When people vote for additional regulation, redistribution, and government spending, it is possible that they may not have even realized that there is another option, and that government decisions from the past can be reversed. The erroneous decision may not even have been identified yet.

It is also important to note that, over decades, decisions to, let's say, subsidize highways or interfere in capital markets create constituencies in favor of maintaining the subsidies and regulations. These are not only government bureaucracies and politicians who engage in pork-barrel politics, but also car producers and middle-class suburbanites in one case, easy-going financial bureaucracies in another, and entrenched management and ministries of culture in still another. However, maintaining these subsidies and institutions has the effect of accumulating mistakes, which is detrimental to prosperity.

How do we quickly rectify long-lasting mistakes? How do we know which intervention is a second-best option and which is simply another costly intervention? Frequently today we just do not know, because there are many regulations on the books—some decades or even centuries old—and the fiscal and regulatory systems are extremely complex. One solution would be to drastically simplify taxes and regulations. The problem with this solution is that most politicians do not want to hear about it. Since they are in the business of selling fiscal and regulatory loopholes, simplicity diminishes their power. It is not surprising that Hong Kong is the only place where an approximation of a flat tax came into being. Another solution would be to enforce a rule that bars additional fiscal or regulatory changes unless at least one that is already on the books is taken off.

If neither of these options is pursued, each tax and each additional regulation may turn out to add costs. Unless there are lucky breaks—such as the successful commercialization of innovations—to cover the costs of these mistakes, governments are forced—eventually—to cut spending.

But when? At what point?

The answers, as shown in this chapter, are that it depends on the checks and balances that exist within a particular country, and on how easily human capital can move out, thus diminishing a government's power to tax and forcing it to speed up the process of rectifying its policies.

CONCLUSION

Talking about "democracy" in the abstract does not bring us closer to solving problems, and also eliminates from the discussion all other kinds of thinking about those problems—even thinking about what exactly the problem is. I hope this book will help restore some balance and reorient the debate.

The historian Donald Kagan once wrote the following about the role of the democratic leader: "Whatever the nobility of his vision and the excellence of his goals, they cannot be achieved in a free society unless the people truly share and are inspired to accomplish them. . . . Any successful society must be an educational institution. However great its commitment to individual freedom and diversity, it needs a core of civic virtue and a general devotion to the common enterprises without which it cannot flourish and survive."

The much-maligned financial markets may not sound like the ideal candidate around which to rally. But remember the metaphor of the farm and the water: just as farms cannot survive and thrive without water, so people cannot thrive or hope to succeed without access to capital. No matter how smart and well-trained a person may be, if capital markets are closed to him he will have to work either for the government or for those privileged few who have access to credit. It is time to find inspiration in the hopes that only the democratization of capital can provide.

There would be no better way to get there than to drastically simplify regulations and the tax system. That would make the political system far more transparent, facilitating our ability to correct mistakes faster. It would lead to the better allocation of talent, to the greater democratization of capital. How can this happen? Once one country bets on it and outshines others, the societies that are falling behind will follow suit. The question is (and we will answer it in the concluding chapter of this book), Which society will be the first to make the radical change?

CHAPTER 3

GLOBALIZATION: THE LONG ROAD FROM IMMOBILITY TO MOBILITY

Should one invest in Mexico? In Russia? The Czech Republic? Thailand? Malaysia? Brazil? Should one buy a company there? Or should one invest only money? In debt? Equity? And for how long? And should one move to work temporarily or permanently in Monterrey, Mexico? In Singapore? Budapest?

The word "globalization" means that we can raise these questions, even if there are still many regulatory obstacles to such movements. Raising these questions means that people have the option of moving themselves, their money, or both in response to opportunities. Globalization means mobility.

Do you want to know where Mexico is in this new global world? More than 10 percent of Mexico is in the U.S. already. Why? Because there are ten million U.S. citizens of Mexican origin, and Mexico's population is one-hundred million. Ten percent of Mexicans have moved—and they prosper far more in the U.S. than their countrymen who stayed behind.

But in truth, much more than 10 percent of Mexico is in the U.S. It's the more determined, entrepreneurial, younger citizens who left. Let's make a rough approximation. If the average yearly income of the ten million expatriates is $20,000, discounted at, say, 5 percent, it represents a wealth of roughly $400,000. Multiply that by 10 million, and the value of human capital realized within the U.S. comes to roughly $4 trillion (or would if Mexico offered comparable opportunities to its people, which it does not).

And if one asked where Cuba is in this New World Order, the answer would be Florida. In the year 2000, Florida is also where Colombians and Venezuelans with higher skills are moving. And where is Beirut? It's in Paris and Montreal. And where is Montreal? In Toronto. Why do we see all this movement? The answer is simple and similar in these cases: politics and taxes drive skilled and entrepreneurial people out of one place and induce them to move to places with greater opportunities.

However, we recall that since the First World War and until just ten years ago, such questions had less meaning. Most countries were closed to the movement of people and capital. China, Russia, and Eastern Europe were Communist, and did not allow their citizens to move. Latin America was recovering from countless military coups; Asia was recovering from wars, disastrous cultural experiments, or both.

To understand the problems that arise with globalization—with the increased mobility of people and capital, that is—we must first look at the features of a world that was less mobile. As the story unfolds, one can see that many of the debates about globalization today reflect the conflict between the actions and outlooks of two groups: the immobile society, represented by politicians, the military, the bureaucracy, immobile industries, and people specialized in such industries; and the mobile society, represented by the skilled, the entrepreneurs, the traders, and the financiers.

LAND, IMMOBILITY, AND POLITICAL POWER

We recall that the main feature of agrarian societies is their immobility. In these societies—as in all societies before the Industrial Revolution and much of the world still today—the riches were derived from land. Wealth was derived from the land. Peasants learned over centuries the minute details of cultivating these lands, of adjusting to changes in weather and conditions of the soil. This knowledge is frequently so place-specific that it's no surprise that the concept of "defending one's land" meant far more to farmers than it did to "traders." What can a farmer who specializes in tropical plants and knows only the nuances of weather patterns in the tropics do in the snowy Midwest? In contrast, traders, international ones in particular, have global networks, and people specialized in technology know no boundaries.

In a world where wealth is derived from agriculture and natural resources (whether gold, oil, forests, or waterfalls), the control of territories, of land, must be insured. Controlling territories means protecting, acquiring, exploiting, and administering them. Without such controls, another country's army will capture the place. In such societies, the institutions, values, culture—indeed their whole outlook—are shaped by these conditions.

Aristocracies and landed gentries, armed forces and police, government ministries and their bureaucracies—all came into existence to provide protection in one place, and, at times, to impose threats and extortions on other similarly immobile societies. They did so by means of an early variation on what one would today call leveraged buyouts—that is, rulers promised soldiers future incomes from captured lands. I call such expeditions a variation on the modern-day leveraged buyout because the comparison is not exact. There were rulers who captured lands, lowered taxes, and gave more freedoms to people in occupied lands, increasing both revenues and taxes. In such instances—Napoleon pursued this strategy for a while—the comparison is accurate. Other rulers had slavery and plunder in their plans, making themselves richer and the largely immobile population in the occupied lands poorer. In the latter case, the comparison is not valid. This was the Islamic model of expansion, and its influence waned.

In agricultural societies, or in societies depending on natural resources, a weak prince, a weak king, or a weak president left his subjects and resources at the mercy of rivals. That is why people were ready to pay taxes—call it protection money, if you wish—to maintain a military force to protect their land and natural resources. The amount people willingly pay for such protection must roughly equal the cost of their moving to a different area, out of both the plunderers' and the tax authorities' reaches. Taxes—or regulations, which are their equivalent—become exorbitant when rulers know that people have nowhere to move.

Since antiquity, kings, feudal lords, dictators of all persuasions understood this very well, and they saw the relationship between the areas they controlled and those controlled by others as hostile. One's gain of territory was another's loss. Approximately, it was a world of zero-sum games.

The rulers also knew that the fewer were people's options to move, the greater was their power to tax. It is not surprising, therefore, to observe throughout history and well into our own times that many governments have done everything in their power to limit the movement of their constituents, and to condemn any trade or any group in society that drew its power from mobility. Merchants, traders, bankers, people dabbling in technology, and financiers had inferior status in these societies for centuries—usury laws, as noted in chapter 1, were an early means of rationalizing such status, with those in the priesthood teaching the convenient mythologies.

India's caste system reflected a similar frame of mind. The *bania,* or businessman, is placed third in the four-caste hierarchy, behind the *brahmins* (priests, teachers, intellectuals—the myth-justifying and -preserving class) and the *kshatryias* (landholders, warriors, rulers), and one step ahead of the *shudras* (laborers).

Look at such typical evidence from another angle. In mainly agrarian societies, some work the land, some go into the army, a fraction goes into either government bureaucracy or the Church, and an even smaller fraction goes to trade. People are defined by their status: as serfs, as landowners, as soldiers, as priests, as traders. Rights and obligations are connected to one's status, are inherited, and are not subject to negotiation. The idea of individual rights—meaning the idea of negotiating rights and obligations that are unconnected to the status one was born to in life—does not exist. Yet it is the idea of contractual law—the freedom to contract unless explicitly prohibited—that allows ordinary people to use their talents, skills, and creativity. It is the freedom to contract that allows people to rely on their initiative and enterprise to bring ideas to life and commercialize them.

At the same time, there is nothing more threatening to the institutions of immobile societies—which are based on the idea that contracts are a matter of status and hierarchy, and that everything is prohibited unless explicitly permitted—than demands to move toward the idea of contractual law. It is difficult to escape perceptions shaped over centuries by institutions adjusted to immobility. Whether this happens because of the self-interest of those in power or because of genuine confusion—the effect of long-taught mythologies—is a marginal issue. Deeds are far more important than motives, which myths and the veils of language can disguise wonderfully, anyway.

When defaults, or their threat, pressure the institutions of immobile societies into moving toward commercialization, what happens—as the examples of Russia, Indonesia, Thailand, and several Latin American countries show—is, first, the development of a kind of caricature of commercial society, a modern variation on the "cargo cults" (discussed in chapter one).

If capitalism means freedom to contract, why not buy a judge or a minister? Why not contract the Mafia to force competitors out of business? Why can't the *nomenklatura* of the once-closed society buy up the assets when their society is suddenly open? And if capitalism is not about freedom to contract, then why can't the government prohibit short selling, as Malaysia's prime minister did following the 1998 Asian crisis? The evolution of institutions to ensure accountability takes a long time.

Rulers have always singled out mobile capital markets in their attacks. They understand that there is nothing that weakens their power more. One should expect that an elite, drawing its power as it does from immobility, will be hostile toward professions that undermine such powers, and that this same elite will exaggerate the benefits of immobility. All these slow the emergence of institutions that would help a society adjust to greater mobility. Again, these policies may be a result of either self-interest or genuine, long-lasting confusion. In either case, they stand in the way of the development of that trust that all laws will be applied equitably to all participants over a long time horizon, which (as I emphasized in chapter one) lays the foundation for democratized capital markets.

It is no surprise, then, that governments in countries endowed with natural resources can sustain mythologies praising immobility, use power to keep their societies immobile, and prevent capital markets from developing. Let us see how.

WEALTH AND RICHES

If once it was true that lands, mines, farms, gold, and oil were the source of wealth in most of the world, this is no longer the case today. The ability to produce wealth by commercializing ideas is far more important than acquiring wealth from land or the occasional high prices of exportable natural resources. However, in societies endowed with natural resources, a powerful elite can sustain itself longer with outdated notions about the nature of wealth—what it is and how it is created—and maintain backward-looking institutions, keeping their societies immobile, frozen.

Let's take, for example, Mexico and Venezuela, Brazil and Kenya, Nigeria, Cameroon, Zaire, and Angola. All are rich in land, mines, oil, diamonds, beaches, safari parks. Occasionally these countries got high revenues from their natural resources. But these windfalls were not used to establish the framework to move toward a mobile, commercial society. Instead, they subsidized a corrupt elite, which used the rents from resources to keep their people immobile, bribing some and forcing others into obedience. Zaire of the 1970s illustrates the many shapes and forms such corruption takes.

Zaire had a quarter of the world's copper reserves. With the price of copper high, and President Richard Nixon praising Zaire's future, the banks forwarded credit to President Mobutu Sese Seko. With so much easy cash available, he splurged on regal estates, jumbo aircraft, five hundred British double-decker buses, and even put money aside in Swiss banks—all while Zaire stayed one of the poorest countries in the world. When the price of copper plummeted, Zaire stopped paying the debt. The banks, having the loans on the books, extended credit. When the debt became $3 billion in 1979, exports (half of which went through Mobutu's family and friends) helped make the payments. Still, the country stayed poor.

Today, Zaire, Sierra Leone, and the "democratic" Republic of Congo fight over diamonds. Oil-rich Nigeria is no different. Its former dictator, Sani Abacha, is believed to have diverted $2 billion during his tenure, of which $1.2 billion was recently discovered in bank accounts in Switzerland and Luxembourg. And today, Nigeria, as well as Cameroon and Angola, finances its wars with neighbors with revenues from oil and diamonds. If Russia had not been so well endowed with rich agricultural land and other natural resources, it is unlikely that Communism could have survived for as long as it did. There would not have been enough resources to sustain a large military and police force, which is what kept people docile and obedient. (And if the IMF and the World Bank today would refuse to channel money through these dictators and kleptocrats, they could be thrown out of power sooner, too.) In countries too well endowed—or cursed, maybe—with natural riches, governments can continue in their monopolistic role as financial intermediaries, sustaining large militaries and bureaucracies, and preventing capital markets from developing.

Thus an embarrassment of natural riches does not make countries wealthy, nor does a lack prevent them from leapfrogging over their resource-rich rivals. If a country is to prosper, it must rely on developing or attracting "brains." Establishing a climate conducive to the democratization of capital markets is the necessary first step.

It is not surprising, therefore, that South Korea, with no natural resources, prospers. And though Japan is a small island with no arable land, a large population, and no natural resources (in fact, it is well endowed with wealth-destroying disasters), it prospers too. Taiwan, Hong Kong, and Singapore reflect similar patterns. And China, with its one billion people and few natural resources, is making faster adjustments to deal with mobility of capital than Russia, with its better endowment of natural resources.

How did resource-poor societies prosper and leapfrog over others, and do so *quickly?* The answer is simple: they either attracted skilled people quickly or rapidly democratized their capital markets.

WEALTH AND THE MOVEMENT OF PEOPLE

The Netherlands is below sea level and has few natural resources. Yet the Dutch Republic became the miracle of the seventeenth century and has prospered ever since, with Amsterdam the jewel in the crown. The city's rags-to-riches story puzzled observers of the time. The puzzle centered not around Spain's and Portugal's riches, which fit into the "finding treasure" pattern, but around Holland's sudden wealth.

England had the grain, timber, and wool, and France had the vineyards and the salt. Yet the Dutch, lacking all of these, and forced to spend fortunes to build and maintain piles to prevent their towns from sinking into the sea, became exporters of fine clothing. They also became the biggest traders in grain, the builders of better and cheaper ships than England, and the exporters of high-quality salt and wine.

This place's sudden emergence was a result of the fact that the Dutch Republic was the first federal state, tolerant toward all religious practices, the most open society of the times. This attracted people from all over Europe, Jews and Huguenots prominent among them. Amsterdam's population jumped from thirty thousand in 1570 to

215,000 in 1630. The political stability and the greater freedoms also attracted entrepreneurs and traders from around the world. The city saw unprecedented innovations in financial practices, including the world's first stock market, where French, Venetians, Florentines, Germans, Poles, Hungarians, Spaniards, Russians, Turks, Armenians, and Hindus traded not only in stocks but in sophisticated derivatives too. Much of the active capital was either foreign-owned or owned by Amsterdammers of foreign birth. In spite of the prosperity such ownership structure brought about three hundred years ago, the idea of foreign ownership is still anathema to politicians even in a Western-type country such as Canada, which continues to regulate it.

Amsterdam became not only the engine of that new country, but a center of growth whose influence radiated throughout Europe and beyond. This is what the historian Violet Barbour has to say in her book on the seventeenth-century Dutch Republic:

> Where Dutch capital went, there swamps were drained, mines opened, forests exploited, canals constructed, ships built, new industries established, mills turned, and trading companies organized. . . . "It may be said," observed Huet about the year 1694, "that the Dutch are in some respects masters of the commerce of the Swedish kingdom since they are masters of the copper trade. The farmers of these mines, being always in need of money, and not finding any in Sweden, pledge this commodity to merchants who advance them the necessary funds." . . . [The Dutch] were capitalist entrepreneurs who raised the commercial and industrial potential of the countries whose resources they developed. An authority on the economic history of Sweden in the seventeenth century has said: "Dutch immigrants dominated almost everything that was new in the economic life of Sweden at the time."

The same was true of Norway, Denmark, Russia, and many other parts of Europe and beyond, where people from Amsterdam brought information about trading opportunities and raised the money to finance them. Amsterdam's entrepreneurs and traders, like those of the Italian city-states before, thought "globally" before anyone bothered to use the term. Today, the difference is that the costs of transportation and communication are significantly lower, and it is the U.S. that plays a role similar to the Dutch Republic's.

It is misleading to say that this was a "Dutch" miracle, however. The openness of the new republic attracted to Amsterdam skilled immigrants, merchants, and moneymen with networks around the world. They were the ones who turned Amsterdam into the financial and trading center of the seventeenth-century world. This was not the case of illiterate Dutch fishermen of the time suddenly becoming financial experts.

Later, Hamburg prospered when the displaced Huguenots moved there at the beginning of the eighteenth century, and when refugees from the French Revolution arrived at the end of that century. Other places in the world went through similar changes. The colonial administrator Sir Stamford Raffles designed Singapore as a port at the beginning of the nineteenth century, and backed it with strong administrative, legal, and education systems, the latter being offered to all members of its multiracial population. From a small settlement, Singapore rose, attracting Chinese, Malays, and Europeans. Trade and security brought prosperity to the penniless emigrants from Indonesia and, in particular, China.

Taiwan (after the seventeenth century), Singapore, and Hong Kong offered newcomers opportunities denied them by the Chinese hinterland, which was dominated at first by warlords and status-conscious bureaucrats and later by Communists. Hong Kong particularly benefited from waves of migrants from China. The city prospered from the inflow of Shanghai merchants and financiers that occurred when Mao Zedong "liberated" China in 1949—much the same way that Amsterdam benefited when Antwerp's merchants and financiers fled the Spanish in earlier centuries. This pattern was repeated when the Huguenots fled France, when the Jews fled many parts of Europe both pre- and post-war, and when

Toronto became home to legions of English-speaking Montrealers fleeing the specter of an independent, tribal Quebec.

Emigrants from Shanghai initiated Hong Kong's textile and shipping industries. They also established a network of merchants, traders, moneymen, and manufacturers—as Jewish, Italian, Armenian, Parsee, and other migrant groups did throughout history in various parts of the world. The resulting entrepreneurial ventures were carried out under the auspices of the British Empire's laws and institutions.

In the 1960s, when Singapore split from Malaysia, Indonesia threatened both countries. However, since the beginning of the 1990s, Indonesia has allowed Singaporean companies to decant some of their labor-intensive operations into some of Indonesia's poorer economies, including Batam Island, where 150 Singapore-based companies have made investments. The island has prospered. But does it mean that it could prosper without the knowledge of Singapore peoples? The answer is no. The combination of critical masses of talent with open capital markets has brought prosperity to some places quickly, a prosperity whose effects were later felt elsewhere. Once in place, these mobile talents have often helped sustain prosperity for generations by attracting new waves of skilled people.

In a 1995 book, *World Class: Thriving Locally in the Global Economy*, Rosabeth Moss Kanter gives examples of the domestic consequences of such mobility:

> In every case, new possibilities are brought to a city by a flow of new people, often outsiders with different ideas and international connections. . . . Consider the role that students, exiles, foreign-born professionals, and foreign companies have played in bringing capital, ideas, or standards to places. . . . This influx of fresh know-how then combined with classic American strength to produce even higher performance; both Japanese-owned Honda in Marysville [Ohio] and Swiss-owned Rieter of

> Spartanburg [South Carolina] eventually outperformed
> units in their parents' country, and Americans became
> the teachers. . . . Looking inward will not help locals
> join the world class; they must also reach outward. To
> do this effectively, with a coherent strategy, requires a
> second ingredient of world-class cities: social glue.

A similar sequence of events is taking place before our eyes. It would be a mistake to attribute the growth of China only to what is happening there without reference to the fact that 55 million expatriate Chinese are involved in 75 percent of the investments, bringing their knowledge and contacts to the mainland.

To recap: the rapid movement of human capital brings prosperity quickly to a place. Financial capital then follows the human one. Globalization has been going on for centuries, even if nobody bothered to use the term—though, of course, information flowed more slowly during the seventeenth century than it does today.

A Post–Second World War Miracle
The post–Second World War West German miracle fits this pattern too, though in popular memory this country's rapid success is associated with the Marshall Plan. This is a false memory about the impact of government aid that governments have an incentive to sustain. The impact of that aid has been greatly exaggerated.

Economists have estimated that from 1948 to 1950, Marshall Plan aid amounted to 5 to 10 percent of the European gross national product (GNP), though these numbers must be taken with a grain of salt. European statistics from those years may seriously underestimate national incomes because of price regulation, extensive black markets, and savage, confiscatory taxation (about which more is said below), and thus could dramatically overestimate the Marshall Plan's impact.

The fact that the influence of the Marshall Plan may be much smaller than mythologies imply can also be inferred from other evidence. After the end of the First World War, aid and loans to Europe were also estimated to amount to about 5 percent of its

70

GNP—yet no miracles happened. True, the world moved toward lower tariffs after the Second World War, which it did not after the First World War. There was also the impact of the disastrous Treaty of Versailles, which failed to establish incentives for European countries to create wealth. Under the terms of the treaty, most of what Germany created would have been paid out to France and England. But if this accounts for the difference, the correct conclusion would be that the post–Second World War miracle is linked to lowered tariffs and a better treaty, rather than to foreign aid.

What are the facts behind the German miracle? Again, mobility of human capital and lower taxes played significant roles. Up to 1961, West Germany accepted 12 million mostly well-trained immigrants, some of whom were forced to leave Poland and Czechoslovakia immediately after the Second World War, and others who later left the "promise" of East Germany's Communist paradise. The importance of this movement can be inferred from the significantly higher ratio of active to total population in West Germany relative to the rest of Europe in the 1950s and 1960s. This ratio stood at 50 percent in Germany but only 45 percent in France, 40 percent in the U.K., 42 percent in the U.S., and 36 percent in Canada.

When the inflow of human capital from Eastern Europe stopped, the Mediterranean lands began supplying new waves of young, ready-made employees who already possessed skills that West Germany did not have to pay them to acquire. In other words, the West German miracle was a result not so much of foreign aid, but of the same features that brought about earlier and later miracles elsewhere: the migration of skilled people, significantly lower income taxes, and lower tariffs (that is, significantly lower taxes on the international movement of goods).

In Germany of 1948, marginal taxes stood at 50 percent for a $600 annual income and a confiscatory 95 percent for an income of $15,000. In 1948, the government lowered taxes drastically: the 50 percent rate kicked in with an annual income of $2,250, though income could be lowered with numerous deductions for savings and investments. By 1955, the top rate was lowered to 63 percent for incomes of more than $250,000, and the 50 percent brackets started at $42,000.

So what brings about economic miracles? The recipe seems to call for countries to maintain low taxes and attract people with brains while the rest of the world experiments with disastrous policies that tax people's hopes, aspirations, and ambitions.

The Scottish Miracle

The Scottish lesson, though it's rarely mentioned in history books, shows how miracles can happen when institutions are rapidly adjusted and capital markets are rapidly democratized, even if there is no inflow of talent from the rest of the world.

Scotland of 1750 was a very poor country, one of Europe's poorest. The land was of poor quality, and illiterate people engaged in near subsistence agriculture. There were no navigable rivers; barren mountains and rocky hills hindered communication. The main export at the time was processed tobacco. Yet less than a century later, Scotland had leapfrogged all Western European countries and stood with England at the forefront of the world's industrial nations. Its standard of living by the mid-1800s was the same as England's; in 1750, it had been about half.

How did the Scots do it? The Union of 1707 made Scotland part of England. It came under the auspices of England's tax system, laws, and currency, and it was allowed access to English markets—a mini version of the European Common Market or the North American Free Trade Agreement (NAFTA). The Union also abolished the Scottish Parliament, leaving Scotland without a distinct administration until 1885. That turned out to be a blessing (reminiscent of Hong Kong's later successes under distant British rule) because it ensured that the banking system and financial markets did not become instruments of government finance, resulting in more frequent mismatches.

By 1810, there were forty independent banks in Scotland. The orthodoxy of the times held that banks should lend only if the loans were backed by the security of goods in transit or in process, and even then for no more than ninety days. But the Scottish banks were free to lend for unspecified periods of time, with no requirement that the loans be backed by securities. In essence, the Scottish banks offered the precursors of junk bonds and Grameen Bank's "micro-loans" (these are small loans offered to people without assets or collateral).

Bills of exchange, the main assets of banks in other countries at the time, were the least important for the Scottish banks. Banks advanced most loans to manufacturers and merchants, who got credit backed only by their own signatures with two or more people as sureties. The banks flourished despite tiny reserves (one percent of their liabilities in specie) and irregular financial reports (annual balance sheets were prepared starting in only 1797).

The Scottish financial historian A. W. Kerr captures the specific feature of the country's financial markets: "The comparative immunity from legislative interference which characterized banking in Scotland until the year 1844 had been an unmistakable blessing to the country, and has saved the banks from those vexatious and unnecessary distinctions and restrictions which have hampered and distorted English banking. In Scotland, banking was permitted to develop as the country advanced in wealth and in intelligence. Nay, it was even enabled to lead the nation on the path of prosperity, and to evolve, from practical experience, a natural and healthy system of banking, which would have been impossible under close state control similar to that followed in other countries." The country showed how to become prosperous quickly through trade and finance, unhindered by tariffs but covered by the reliable English political and legal umbrella.

Let's contrast Scotland of those times with France, where until 1857 the Conseil d'État (state council) rejected a majority of the requests for charters for financial institutions. A severe depression that year, however, led to the liberalization of procedures. Necessity is the mother of invention in the political sphere too. Yet even in 1870, banking services in France were not what they had been in Scotland at the beginning of that century, and regulations denied small industrialists access to credit.

Scotland stands out not only because of its unique banking system, but also because of the emphasis it put on education during

Capital
Connections

the early part of the eighteenth century. The Scots understood the importance of not only democratized capital markets, but also human capital. One hundred years after the union with England, between 1800 and 1850, the output of outstanding Scottish scientists was at its height.

But there are other lessons to be drawn from the Scottish case, besides the importance of having access to capital, both financial and human. Personal savings were certainly not a precondition for Scottish prosperity. The Scots did not have any to speak of, and nor did they get any foreign aid. But once opportunities were open and financial markets were allowed to develop relatively unhindered, the Scots were able to borrow against future incomes and invest. And the amounts borrowed were put to much better use in Scotland than in any other country. Entrepreneurs did not have to rely on the government to be their financial intermediary. Indeed, this was the key to Scottish prosperity, for, unlike the other miracle countries we've examined, Scotland was not the beneficiary of any large-scale movement of talent from elsewhere in the world.

Why Do Talents Move Out Slowly, and What Happens When They Move Out?

Let's turn our attention to New York and London. They have become financial centers, and have continued to dominate financial services in spite of periods of occasional high taxation, high costs of living, increased crime rates, and deteriorating infrastructures. Half of the world's largest banks by asset value, two-thirds of the net income of those banks, and virtually all of the world's twenty-five largest securities firms are based in these two cities and in Tokyo. When a niche developed in those markets, it too became concentrated in one of a few places: futures and derivatives trading in Chicago, fund management in Boston, insurance in Hartford, Connecticut.

Why is it that once critical masses of talent have settled in a place, they are slow to leave when governments pursue mistaken policies? The answer is that such critical masses represent a whole network of jobs and colleagues, and allow for narrow specialization. Once a person has specialized, her wealth is linked to the network's. If she moves, she loses the benefits of her specialization. A simple example, the film industry, makes this clear. If screenwriters, directors, and producers move, the specialized technical staff linked to the industry has to choose between staying and changing jobs or moving too. What will a specialized stuntman do if the rest of the movie industry moves out? It's no surprise, therefore, that the migration of a vital few is followed by either a massive exodus or, if the masses cannot follow the vital few, a significant drop in standards of living.

The first possibility explains why London, New York, and Frankfurt have stayed financial centers; Milan and Paris centers of fashion, design, furniture, and advertising; Hollywood the center for film and entertainment—even when these industries face draconian taxes or other adversity. Once there is a large pool of talent in place, even disastrous fiscal policies may not lead to the immediate decline of a city, a region, or a country. People either find ingenious ways to circumvent these taxes, be it through black markets or bribes (in Italy's case), or they make sacrifices for a while, hoping that the adverse times will pass. They'll wait as long as others are waiting as well. However, once people start moving, the ripple suddenly turns into a wave—as has been Canada's experience in recent years. At this stage, the city, the region, or the country declines. Canada, with its failure to adopt policies designed to retain the vital few, is a good example of a country that has been going through this process during the past few decades—despite Ottawa's spin doctors' attempts to rename the "brain drain" a "brain loan."

WHAT IS ONE TO DO?

Politicians and economists promise growth, prosperity, and higher standards of living. But the fastest way to realize these goals, as this chapter shows, is to attract critical masses of talent to a place, and at the same time rapidly open up financial markets (as the Scottish case exemplified). Governments around the world, of all stripes, would be forced to correct their mistakes more quickly if it was easier for people to move across borders. Citizens then would see their most talented countrymen leaving for fairer shores. This is one reason many governments oppose the free movement of people. When people can vote with their feet, they quickly reveal their governments' mistakes, and thus diminish their power to tax and regulate. Indeed, if Western governments are genuinely interested in changing other countries' oppressive regimes, they can do no better than to open up their own borders for migration.

Once societies have open capital markets and borders, it will be easier to see which policies bring about prosperity and which ones do not. Changes in the total market value of firms (the value of stocks added to the value of outstanding debt), when added to the value of government debt (all in terms of a monetary standard), are the best indicator. When this figure increases, it means that the society's ability to generate revenues and pay back debt—whether private or public—has improved. When this sum drops, it's a signal to people that their government is making erroneous decisions. When this happens, investors quickly redirect capital among other countries, and thus ensure better matches between people and that capital.

An important caveat is that for financial markets to be able to signal growth, they must have proper "depth." A historical reminder makes this point clear. In the second half of the nineteenth century, American stock markets saw spectacular booms and spectacular busts. Why? For one thing, channels of information were few. Those who had access to information did not always have an incentive to tell the truth, and in fact often had incentives to collude. Not surprisingly, those without access to privileged information withdrew from the markets. As a result, the markets lacked depth.

Charles Dow, Edward Jones, and Charles Bergstresser saw the problem and came up with a solution: they began publishing a financial newsletter in 1880. That eventually led to the 1895 proposal for a U.S. stock exchange, to the radical innovation of published annual reports, and, of course, to the still-existing Dow Jones company and brand name. The financial information Dow, Jones, and company provided one hundred years ago was carried through New York's streets from offices to banks—albeit by couriers on foot rather than by data flowing through satellites, cables, and optical fibers.

It was no accident that cities with stock exchanges also saw the emergence of a critical mass of people specializing in the information industry: newspaper people, broadcasters, financial and political analysts. It's this information industry that allows capital markets to acquire the proper depth. Such adjustments take time, of course, but this chapter has shown ways in which that period can be condensed (by attracting skilled people and pursuing policies conducive to the democratization of capital markets).

The link with the movement of people brings us back to where we started. When governments pursue mistaken policies and total market capitalizations diminish, where does the wealth go? Does it just disappear? In countries where both capital and people have only a limited ability to move, the diminished value is a permanent loss. Those things that are expected to be solid—people's efforts and ingenuity, for example—melt into thin air. People make less effort, ideas stay in people's heads or on paper, and investors expect more numerous and long-lasting mismatches. The decrease in market capitalization thus reflects slower growth.

When capital and people can move, though, the wealth that disappears in one country reappears in others. There are few better examples to illustrate this point than the wealth created by the various diaspora—Armenian, Chinese, Huguenot, Jewish, and so on— seemingly out of the blue. The movement of the most gifted and energetic of these people led to many of the world's economic "miracles," as shown in this chapter.

It is a big mistake to regard Silicon Valley's success as an example of the importance of high-tech industries, with the idea that such success then can be emulated by the simple transference of technical know-how. One-third of Silicon Valley employees are foreign born, and roughly one-third of CEOs are of Indian origin. Can another country replicate such success without attracting masses of bright, ambitious immigrants? It is doubtful. Open capital markets suggest tolerance of immigrants, of other tribes and cultures (which I'll discuss in more detail in chapter six), and these factors are combined to build up the complex network that is Silicon Valley. Technology is only a part of it.

Economists in the future may calculate exactly how much of the post–Second World War prosperity the United States and the dozen Western democracies have enjoyed can be attributed to the large movement of extremely skilled, ambitious, well-connected people from around the world. Only then will we know how much the transfer of this unmeasured human capital helped cover for many mistaken government policies. What should be clear from the historical evidence is that when and if the rest of the world retains its talents, the dozen Western democracies will no longer be able to count on this method of covering costly mistakes, but instead will have to adopt the Scottish policy to thrive.

CHAPTER 4

DIRECT DEMOCRACY AND FINANCIAL MARKETS: WHAT DO THEY HAVE IN COMMON?

How did the citizens of some countries manage to prevent their governments from pursuing policies that were harmful to prosperity? As we have seen, voting rights were not much of an obstacle to governments intent on doing harm. Instead, democratized capital markets, smaller governments, and more checks and balances— greater accountability, that is—brought superior outcomes.

Many superficial theories argue that U.S. capital markets undermine performance by forcing companies to focus on short-term results. In fact, it is the iron grip of these capital markets that prevents companies from persisting in mistakes. The countries that are in trouble are those where capital markets are unable to play this role, and where governments can escape market control by taxing more and debasing their currency.

Are there better methods than those we already practice that will help us control the size of governments and make them more accountable? In other words, since government is a monopolistic financial intermediary, can we emulate the workings of financial markets in the political sphere and bring in a "guardian" to prevent abuse of power?

An examination of the unique Swiss political system offers one possible answer to these questions. It also provides the opportunity for us to discard the twentieth-century pseudo-science of "macroeconomics," a harmful myth that still shapes the government and central bank policies of many nations, as well as the language of debate surrounding them.

GOVERNMENT SPENDING AND FINANCIAL PRINCIPLES

The value of corporations or governments is determined not by how much money they spend, but by the expected benefits of that spending. In finance, this principle is well known. It explains why stockmarket players pay little attention to book values when evaluating companies. They know that book values are useful only as measures of how much capital investors put *into* a company. Management's success in creating *future* value depends upon its ability to produce adequate returns on the amounts invested.

The stock market continuously renders such judgments on corporations. But who judges the value of government spending? And how frequently? In theory, of course, it is the voting public, through the electoral process. But as we saw in the previous chapters, experience shows that the public has actually had relatively little direct control over government fiscal matters—even within democracies. Also, international capital markets have had only limited success controlling the spending of internally unaccountable governments.

Are there better means of preventing mistaken policies from persisting too long? Can we devise a political counterpart to the stock market that would provide ongoing evaluations of the effectiveness of governments and their fiscal policies? In this chapter, I use the example of Switzerland as evidence that referenda and citizen initiatives can discipline the public sector in much the same way that the stock market disciplines the private sector.

A referendum ensures that resolutions made by representatives are submitted to the people for acceptance or rejection. Citizen initiative means that people have the right not only to vote on proposals, but also to *initiate* new laws or constitutional amendments, and to alter and abolish old ones. Referenda and initiatives—often referred to collectively as direct democracy—act to discipline governments at all levels by separating the powers to tax and to spend. Such institutions cannot guard against occasional mistakes, however. Nothing can. But by giving the public veto power over specific spending proposals, direct democracy can prevent mistaken policies from lasting too long.

To use another financial metaphor, referenda and initiatives would act as the political equivalent of "project financing"—that is, a means of evaluating and funding projects on a stand-alone basis. By forcing more projects to stand on their own merits, we could put an end to the present political "log-rolling" process, in which legislative compromises routinely sacrifice the larger public wishes to an array of special interests. We could also counteract the effects of the language of so-called macroeconomic theory, which labels government spending as "investment" even when it's really just pork-barrel politics or, worse still, outright corruption. A move toward such a form of democracy requires a "linguistic" revolution first. We must rid ourselves of the false language and mythologies that presently shape public policy and lead societies into mazes of error. Words bias thought—and public debates.

GOVERNMENT SPENDING AND MACROECONOMIC THEORY

There is no such thing as a "general theory" that will provide reliable answers to all of today's most commonly asked questions, such as:

- How does the general level of a government's spending, in particular its debts and deficits (or even its surpluses), affect the total production of goods and services or the national income earned from production?

81

- How do debts and deficits affect employment?
- How do debts and deficits affect the allocation of resources between consumption and investment?

There's a simple reason why no general answers can be given to any of these questions. An increase in any one of government spending, debts, or deficits can have a positive, negative, or neutral effect on national income, employment, or interest rates. Increased deficits may increase current consumption levels and diminish investments, for example, or they may not. It all depends on what the government does with the money, and how accountable this government is. In other words, the answer depends on institutional details.

The abstract, aggregate language of macroeconomics does not pay any attention to these details, or to the matching issue discussed in previous chapters. As we saw in those chapters, prosperity comes when accountable institutions match money and people. When institutions are less accountable, more mismatches happen, and those that do happen last longer. Mismatches lower standards of living, since every mismatch is a cost (even if governments call it an "investment," and raise taxes and accumulate deficits to pay for it, making the effects less visible).

If we make better matches, we are not only using capital more effectively, but also increasing the returns people can expect on their savings. People can save less in a country where better matches are made, since they can expect higher returns (this is the magic of compounded returns). If the average return in the U.S. is, say, 10 percent (but it's only 5 percent in, for example, France), this compensates for much lower savings rates among American citizens—another variable totally misinterpreted by macroeconomists.

The U.S.'s frequently maligned financial markets in fact play the crucial role in this matching process. More often than not, they create the better matches by insisting on one clear, simple, and focused objective: financial performance. If firms don't perform, their funds become more costly. It's that simple. Though some politicians and economists claim that capital markets force firms to focus on short-term results, the evidence is quite the contrary. Take a look at the patience capital markets have displayed with Amazon.com and other Internet companies, for example, or go back a few decades and examine the treatment of the early entrants in wireless communication, such as McCaw Cellular (which was bought for billions by AT&T, though it had no history of profitability at the time of the purchase).

The suggestion here is not that politicians and bureaucrats are incompetent. But even if these people were as highly skilled in making investment decisions as their private-market counterparts in other countries—which is unlikely to be the case, since, having no experience, they generally lack an understanding of the details of managing and financing businesses—the level of accountability is not the same. Bureaucrats and politicians do not personally go bankrupt if they make disastrous matches. Often, they are not even held accountable. This is not to say that venture capital firms, banks, and other financial institutions never make mismatches when allocating capital. They do. But they cannot afford to make very many mistakes, and they do not have the luxury of correcting their mistakes slowly. Governments, on the other hand, can make many more and greater mistakes, and also fail to correct them. They then can cover their mistakes by taxing, borrowing, inflating, and devaluing their currency. These methods of financing government spending—none of which is available to private financial institutions, thank heavens—allow mismatches to persist.

When we view government as a special financial intermediary with degrees of monopoly powers, we shed light not only on why macroeconomics, with its generalized language, misleads, but also on why Japan does not perform well (the beloved "high savings" macroeconomic theory notwithstanding). It also explains, in part, what makes Europe and the Euro sick, why Canada has been falling behind the U.S., why the U.S. needn't worry even though its citizens save relatively little, and why questions on how to spend "the surplus" are the wrong ones to ask if we want to understand what makes countries prosper or fall behind.

The question we should be asking is this: Who can make better matches between money and talent—bureaucrats and politicians who are subject to elections only occasionally, or their private-market counterparts, who are held accountable for their matching and mismatching decisions every split second?

It's important, then, to realize that we cannot add up all government spending and discuss the impact of the sum total on prosperity (as macroeconomists do); part of the sum might have been wisely invested, another part wasted. Indeed, there have been many statistical analysis that attempted to discover and quantify relationships between government spending, deficits, and various aggregates. But as one would expect, such studies have provided no clear answers. Deficits have not been shown to be systematically related to higher inflation, higher interest rates (either nominal or real), or lower private investments.

Since some readers may justly say that there is no smoke without fire, let's turn to a fundamental question: Where does this wrong-headed macroeconomic approach, whose language has so captured the public discourse over the past few decades, come from?

KEYNES AND THE FALLACY OF AGGREGATION

Why did economists add up the different spending to start with? And why did they think such aggregate sums—independent of politics, regulations, or institutions to ensure accountability— were relevant to predicting where a society was heading?

The false language that surrounds debates about debts, deficits, surpluses, unemployment, and currency matters today is still a legacy of John Maynard Keynes's *General Theory of Employment, Interest and Money,* published in 1936, when the Western world was facing unprecedented rates of unemployment. Keynes was the first economist to suggest that we should look at the level (and not the specific type) of government spending and deficits to explain macroeconomic behavior. He suggested that increases in deficits, public debts, and government spending can be used systematically by governments to prevent troubled times. This argument has since been revealed, by the experience of many national economies, to be wrong in general, even though its policy implications happened to be right during the 1930s.

Keynes's theory worked in the Depression era because of its particular circumstances, as noted in chapter one. The mistake came when later generations thought that since the policies had worked then, they would work always and everywhere, that indeed they constituted a general theory. Many prominent economists of the time agreed with Keynes that in the 1930s, spending money on public works—turning government into a financial intermediary, that is—even if it was just to dig "holes in the ground" (as Keynes puts it), was a solution. Indeed, even his critics did not disagree with Keynes's belief in the occasional usefulness of public works, though some objected to both the definitions and the theories Keynes put forward to justify such spending. What troubled most, however, was Keynes's elitist suggestion that depressions will routinely occur in decentralized economies unless—hold your breath again—politicians (with the help of their economic advisers) intervene to "manage demand."

What, in Keynes's view, are the causes of increased unemployment (during the 1930s, in particular), and why should governments intervene by spending on public works? Although decreased levels of consumption and a rise in interest rates can lead to such outcomes, Keynes attributes the problem to a "sudden collapse in the marginal efficiency of capital"—low returns from investments, that is. Once expectations have fallen, Keynes adds, they are:

> not easy to revive, determined as [they are] by the uncontrollable and disobedient psychology of the business world. It is the return of confidence, to speak in ordinary language, which is so insusceptible to control in an economy of individualistic capitalism. This is the aspect of the slump which bankers and businessmen have been right in emphasizing, and which the economists who have put their faith in a "purely monetary" remedy have underestimated.

This view leads Keynes to his conclusion that public works—government-financed employment programs, in other words—even those of doubtful utility, will pay for themselves over and over again at a time of severe unemployment. There is not even a hint in Keynes's work that such a collapse could be triggered by the mistaken policies of governments or central banks (as we saw in previous chapters).

To support this conclusion, Keynes reminds readers that such policies have been pursued since ancient times:

> Pyramid buildings, . . . even wars, may serve to increase wealth, if the education of our statesmen on the principles of the classical economics stands in the way of anything better. . . . Just as wars have been the only form of large-scale loan expenditure which statesmen have thought justifiable, so gold-mining is the only pretext for digging holes in the ground which has recommended itself to bankers as sound finance. . . . Ancient Egypt was doubly fortunate, and doubtless owed to this its fabled wealth, in that it possessed two activities: . . . pyramid building as well as the search for precious metals. . . . The Middle Ages built cathedrals and sang dirges. . . .

From these comments, one can infer that Keynes either did not know much history or did not read it carefully. The policies of those ancient times were not meant to offset those "sudden drops in the marginal efficiency of capital" caused by the caprices of private investors at all, and they had nothing to do with the government becoming a financial intermediary. Instead, they were intended for something entirely different—giving people some hope and a stake in their own societies, or dampening revolutionary ardor. community stake

THE CLASSICAL VIEW OF PUBLIC WORKS

The question of how to deal with the poor is one that many rulers and leaders of governments since antiquity have asked themselves, and one that many writers since ancient times have tried to answer. These writers agreed on the following: the poor, and those falling behind, have less interest in maintaining the status quo when they do not have a stake in the system, and thus these people are also the greatest menace to its maintenance. Having less at stake, they are more prone to violence, more likely to commit crimes against other people's property, and more likely to bet on ideas to rationalize their plunder.

Rulers and politicians have long recognized that spending money to protect property and punish violators is not always the way to keep the populace calm. As we saw in previous chapters, governments that want to keep the majority calm without opening capital markets can themselves become financial intermediaries and rely on other institutions to maintain order. This course of action will, to some extent, sustain hope among the poor without giving up much power (which would have happened with the opening of capital markets).

Keynes's statement on the pyramids echoed the traditional lines of argument of many other English economists. Sir William Petty, a well-known English commentator of the seventeenth century, proposed using tax money for the construction of useless pyramids on Salisbury Plain, as well as for "entertainments, magnificent shews, triumphal arches." His proposal had nothing to do with increasing employment and manipulating investors' expectations in the short run, but everything to do with dealing with the poor in the long run. Seventeenth-century observers were preoccupied with persistent unemployment among the same groups of people (poverty, that is), and they attempted to devise lasting remedies—though without giving up any of their own power.

Petty thought that since the poor must be provided for, it would be better for them (and for society) to be employed and paid, rather than given charity. Even if the work consisted of little more than bringing "the Stones at Stonehenge to Tower Hill," it could "keep their minds to discipline and obedience, and their body to a patience of more profitable labors when need shall require it," lest they lose the faculty of laboring. Petty's view was representative. During the second half of the seventeenth century, all economic and political tracts—Giovanni Botero's classic *The Reason for State* is another typical example—discussed employment and public works in a similar fashion. The general view was that between the dislocation of the past and the expectation for the future, governments must build a bridge for the dependent poor, by either employing them or helping to retrain them. The nature of their employment seemed secondary to some observers, as it also seemed later to Keynes and even to some people today.

Circuses and pyramids, cathedrals, and Paris's famous great boulevards are all examples of public works that were undertaken either to give employment to the poor or to prevent disorders and rebellions. Wider streets give the advantage to police forces and armies, rather than to demonstrators (no wonder large squares can be found in the capital cities of most dictatorial countries—including Moscow, Beijing, St. Petersburg, and the capitals of many Latin American countries—but not in London). In fact, Parisian boulevards were made wide so that a rifle of the times could still shoot revolutionaries on the other side. It was not because Baron Haussmann was visionary and anticipated the twentieth century's cars and tourists, or because he expected that Impressionists would educate our eyes to perceive beauty in the bombastic uniformity of these boulevards.

The great Elizabethan poor laws also sprang from this preoccupation with the maintenance of order and the management of the poor. Though the poor laws were disparaged, most observers were critical only of the way they were administered—rather like popular attitudes toward welfare today. None of the arguments for or against such interventions had to do with short-run policies or temporary unemployment.

Instead, observers held views that ranged between two extremes. Those at one pole of the debate viewed any and all spending on the poor, through public works or otherwise, as beneficial because it gave a stake to those on the bottom, and in the long run helped form a better educated and disciplined population. Those at the other extreme thought such policies undermined long-run prosperity by breeding idleness and a sense of entitlement, and by strengthening existing bureaucracies and creating new ones. The latter group also believed such policies diminished incentives to invest (because they could lead eventually to higher tax rates) and delayed necessary adjustment to change.

As often happens, the truth about public works projects—and about public spending generally—was recognized by most classical economists to lie somewhere between these two extreme views. Societies inherit mistaken regulations and then, seeing their effects but not quite sure what hit them, ask governments to make up for their unintended consequences. But this raises a practical issue: what was the intermediate point at which stabilizing policies—in the aforementioned sense of the word (that is, policies designed to prevent crime and quash rebellions), rather than the narrow meaning used by macroeconomists (those designed to prevent business cycles)—themselves became burdens on prosperity? This question brings us back to the main promise held out by referenda and initiatives—political institutions that do not figure at all in macroeconomics.

In fact, macroeconomic theory, as we saw earlier, though it does address government spending, makes absolutely no reference to political institutions. It uses the same terms and recommends the same policies, whether the country in question is a true democracy, a "cargo cult," or a dictatorship. No wonder the latter governments adopted the theory and its language with great enthusiasm. Macroeconomic theory offered routes to prosperity—without making any reference to the need to open up capital markets or require accountability from governments.

A POLITICAL REMEDY FOR PREVENTING LASTING MISTAKES

Whether investments are truly "investments" depends not on how economists and governments define them, but on whether the tax-paying citizens expect to earn back, directly or indirectly, more than they put in.

Economists can count government spending on infrastructure and education as investment if they please. But a road that is rarely used; an airport that lacks traffic; schools and colleges that graduate illiterate students; and government-sponsored films, books, and pieces of music that are never watched, read, or heard (statistical culture)—none of these provides a return to society that would justify financing them. Although they may be counted as investment, they are nothing of the kind.

Of course, bad investment decisions made by private firms are also counted as investment—for a while. But we emphasized the crucial difference before: mismatches financed by private companies lose money and will be terminated eventually, but government-financed projects have leverage before they default. Governments can raise taxes, borrow funds, and also inflate, options that are not available to private companies. Without the institutions of referendum and initiative, people have limited control over both the type and amount of government spending, since they can vote only infrequently.

How, then, can societies decide how much to spend on, say, health care, education, or infrastructure? Are these expenditures "investments," or are they moneys misspent? But let's even say that the government can match money wisely and prudently on health care, the environment, education, the arts, and other "worthy" causes. No society is rich enough to pay for all these causes. Choices must be made. What is the solution? What is the "right size" for government?

Referenda and initiatives offer long-lasting, stable political solutions to this question.

A Swiss Solution

The Swiss have practiced referenda and initiatives on a national level for more than one hundred years. In fact, the principle of referendum was incorporated into the Swiss federal constitution in 1874 (and on local levels the practice goes back to the Middle Ages). In 1891, an amendment providing for "initiative" was added to the constitution. This stated that people have the right not only to vote on proposals, but also to initiate new laws or constitutional amendments, and to alter or abolish old ones (if at least fifty thousand fellow citizens agree).

This feature is important, for it distinguishes the Swiss system from that of other nations (where politicians only occasionally resort to referenda). In Switzerland, direct democracy is embedded in the constitution. In other countries, referenda are generally used only when politically expedient—as we'll see later. In other words, although the same term is used to describe two very different practices, we should not confuse the occasional plebiscite with the constitutionally guaranteed institutions of the Swiss. The latter system provides a way for systematically correcting mistaken decisions; the irregular, un-guaranteed one does not.

Also, the institution of initiative should not be confused with petitions or lobbying. Politicians in other Western democracies are free to treat petitions as they see fit. They can also respond far too easily to lobbying by special interests. In contrast, Swiss politicians have more difficulty subverting people's will, since their actions can be undone.

It is no accident, therefore, that politicians have limited roles to play in Switzerland, and one does not hear much about them. Nor is it accidental that no significant differences divide the policies of the major political parties. Through these two institutions, the electorate is allowed to vote directly on proposals and issues. This obviates the need for painful compromises during votes on both candidates and legislative "packages." As has become embarrassingly clear in the political jockeying over bills in Western democracies, legislators in other countries who back one measure strongly are regularly forced to vote for measures with which they disagree to gain the reciprocal backing of other legislators. By nullifying such legislative compromises, referenda significantly diminish the power of politicians and bureaucrats, and thus the extent of pork-barrel politics.

Here is a sampling of the issues on which Swiss referenda have been held:

- Citizens voted for proportional voting for Parliament in 1918, even though politicians belonging to the majority Radical-Democratic Party initially rejected the measure. In the next elections, this party lost 40 percent of its seats.
- A popular initiative in 1946 succeeded in making "urgent" federal laws

91

subject to obligatory referenda within one year, though both the government and the opposition were against it.

• Seventy-six percent of Swiss citizens rejected a proposal to join the United Nations, though Parliament was in favor.

In recent years, the Swiss have voted separately on issues such as requiring extra air-pollution devices in motor vehicles, the legalization of abortion and drugs, the introduction of a value-added tax (VAT), and increasing grants for universities and research. All these initiatives were voted down in national referenda. Other initiatives—including those concerning consumer protection and equal rights for women and men, the purchase of airplanes for the military, and the signing of agreements with the European Community (EC)—were accepted. The referenda on the EC reversed the results of an earlier vote, when twenty-three of thirty cantons voted against the proposal.

Altogether, of the 216 amendments proposed between 1874 and 1985 on both the federal and the canton level, 111 were accepted and 105 were rejected. Of the 111 accepted, eight were popular initiatives and fourteen were counter-proposals. On the federal level alone, between 1848 and 1990, there were 147 obligatory referenda (on constitutional issues) and 103 optional ones (on laws), as well as 104 initiatives.

Referenda and initiatives diminish the power of politicians and the influence of bureaucrats, and hence the incentives of lobbying groups to organize. These institutions impose stricter controls on government spending and allow for quicker correction of misguided policies. These combined effects imply a greater alignment between political decisions and voter preferences (without necessarily implying either less taxation or fewer regulations). This is indeed what Swiss researchers found when they looked at the evidence across the cantons.

Consider, then, how such a system would deal with some recent election issues in the United States. Al Gore proposed adding twenty-nine new credits to the tax code. Those eligible for these credits included taxpayers with kids in government-approved day-care centers, taxpayers with kids in college (if they do not earn more than $120,000 a year), and taxpayers who are beneficiaries of an estate (if the estate qualifies as a small business and the beneficiary "materially participates" in that business for five out of eight years following the owner's death). And this was just a minor part of the Democratic platform.

Would politicians even offer such complex schemes if they knew that people had the option of rejecting them? It's doubtful. They would be more likely to put on the table simpler, more focused, separate plans. It is also likely that in the debate preceding a referendum on, say, health care, someone would ask how politicians and bureaucrats can reasonably be expected to price drugs and complex insurance plans when they have no clue how to price simpler products, such as chicken and eggs.

When, under the present system, people vote on a complex bundle that covers everything from health care and education to social security, the end result is the usual package deal of pork-barrel politics.

Consider how large-scale R&D programs were backed, for example. Economists frequently cite the funding of "basic" research as a necessary role of government (since they assume that the private sector will not finance it). Yet in one book, *The Technology Pork Barrel,* Linda Cohen, Roger Noll, and their co-authors find that American R&D programs had proven to be an enormous waste of taxpayer funds. They write:

> On the basis of retrospective benefit-cost analysis, only one program—NASA's activities in developing communication satellites—can be regarded as worth the effort. But that program was killed. . . . The photovoltaics program made significant progress, but it was dramatically scaled back for political reasons. . . . The remaining four programs were almost unqualified failures. The supersonic transport (SST) and Clinch River Breeder Reactor were killed before they produced any benefits, and Clinch River, because of cost overruns, absorbed so much of the R&D budget for nuclear technology that it

> probably retarded overall technological progress. The
> space shuttle . . . costs too much, and flies too infre-
> quently. The synthetic fuels program produced one
> promising technology . . . but billions were spent on an-
> other pilot and demonstration facilities that failed.

The title of the book points to the source of this failure. Once again, referenda and initiatives could provide a remedy. Even if people favored some government role in financing R&D, they could initiate votes on specific programs, forcing failed experiments to be ended and successful ones protected.

As a final example, let us discuss how referenda and initiatives could provide solutions to the social security problem. In a recent book, *Gray Dawn: How the Coming Age Wave Will Transform America—And the World.* Peter Peterson (who served in President Nixon's Cabinet) points out that in 2020, there will be 25 million more people receiving social security than there are today. If benefits are kept at the promised level, this will add $232 billion to the annual American budget. If Medicare is added at the promised level, the picture gets worse.

What are Peterson's solutions? One is to renege on the promise to pay every retiree, as well as to reduce or eliminate all benefits to those with an annual income in excess of US$40,000. Another is to raise the age of retirement. Still others are to replace the present system with one similar to that now practiced in Chile and Singapore (mandatory individual accounts), and to shift from income to consumption taxes. And there are others he does not mention. How about letting in more skilled, young immigrants? (In fact, the U.S. moved in just this direction in 2000, making it easier for the high-tech industry to bring in six-hundred thousand highly skilled immigrants.)

This all tells us that in Western countries today, we have no idea what we are measuring when we look at vastly increased government spending on just health and education. Much of it probably reflects the costs of maintaining a large bureaucracy, as well as the power of lobbying and interest groups, rather than the costs of providing higher-quality programs. Referenda and initiatives (when preceded by debates on the choices) could help control the size of governments at all levels, as well as determining how those governments should be financed. If people make a mistaken choice first, it can be corrected later through initiatives.

It's clear, then, that referenda and initiatives on separate issues would lead to a closer relationship between fact and measurement, between actual well-being and the data that are supposed to reflect it, and would restore power to voters. There is nothing surprising in today's low turnouts during elections: people know that they do not have control over government spending, democratic principles notwithstanding. When people are given the chance to either approve or reject concrete, detailed spending proposals, they vote in greater numbers. They know they can correct situations when preferences change, or when the government's performance leaves something to be desired.

CAN OTHER NATIONS BECOME LIKE SWITZERLAND?

One typical objection to adopting the Swiss system in other countries is that people must first become Swiss before agreeing to them. This may sound funny, but it turns out to be just another play on words. Closer inspection reveals that the Swiss were not so "Swiss" before they agreed to the widespread use of these institutions (though Swiss villages have held town-hall meetings for centuries). Rather, these institutions turned them into the calm, civilized, prosperous, peaceful people we are accustomed to today.

Until the beginning of the nineteenth century, the Swiss had their share of religious conflicts—like all other Europeans. In the 1830s there were protests against aristocratic governments, and in 1831 serious conflicts arose in the cantons of Basle, Schweiz, and Neuchâtel. In 1847 twelve and a half cantons joined the Federal cause, seven joined the Secessionists, and one full and two half-cantons remained neutral. From 1861 to 1864, the Swiss fought their civil war. The Secessionists lost. The subsequent constitutional reforms led to the 1874 document that identifies the current Swiss political system. This document, and the rules it delivered and enforced, forged a federation of German-, French-, and Italian-speakers (and the small number of Romansh) into the current Swiss tribe.

It would be a mistake to think that the tribe ceased to have internal conflicts; in fact, the linguistic ones were troublesome. But these too were solved through a sequence of referenda, though this use of direct democracy was inadvertent. Consider, for example, the carving out of the French-speaking canton of Jura from the German canton of Bern in 1974. Bern's German majority was continuously complaining that the government was spending more on each Juran than it was on other citizens, and that the Jurans were already better off than the average French-Swiss citizen. Eventually, a strong French-Juran separatist movement emerged, although Jurans represented only 7 percent of the canton's population.

According to federal law, a simple majority referendum was not enough to decide on Juran independence. A number of individual referenda had to be held: one for the region of Jura as a whole, one for "border" communities, and others for any district in which 20 percent of the electorate petitioned for it. In 1974, the Jurans gained a small majority (54.2 percent) and got their canton, which was accepted into the confederation in 1978, following a national referendum. In 1975, three French-speaking border districts voted to leave Jura and become part of Bern, but in additional referenda eight border communities voted to join Jura.

Linguistic tensions were not the only ones leading to the redrawing of internal borders. Taxes were another, and this led to the creation of two half-cantons: Basle-Town and Basle-Country. The Basle-Country canton decreased taxes, while the Basle-Town canton increased them. The first prospered; the other lost 13 percent of its population, stagnated, and eventually also reduced taxation. While these events are not common in Swiss history, they are possible. It is their feasibility that checks the powers of the canton governments.

In other words, moving borders on paper, rather than forcing people to move with their feet (a far more costly undertaking), has helped the Swiss to shape the provision of public goods and control their governments' spending habits.

Other Objections

There are several other common objections to the Swiss federal system. One is that the institutions of referendum and initiative are far too costly to operate in more populous countries, such as the United States. But this is not a serious objection in technologically advanced nations. Innovations in communication technologies—today's electronic highways—have dramatically lowered the costs of operating such institutions. In an interconnected nation, problems relating to distance and large populations can be easily and cheaply overcome. At the same time, the costs of large governments and mistaken policies—which might be eliminated by shifting toward referenda and initiatives—have increased. It may turn out that a major (but unintended) benefit of the innovations we've seen over the past decade in communication technology will be the political change they help bring about.

In fact, this is happening already in the United States. In the recent book *Democracy Derailed,* David Broder describes how the system of initiative first arrived in the United States one hundred years ago, and worked well for the first twenty-five. With the two world wars, the Great Depression, and the Cold War, however, the system became a marginal form of lawmaking. This is not surprising: there were far more pressing issues to be addressed, and as we saw in chapter one, capital markets could not serve as a model for reconfigured political institutions.

The initiative process came back in 1978 with California's famous Proposition 13, which cut property taxes from about 2.5 percent of market value to one percent. Within two years, forty-three other states had implemented property-tax limitations, and fifteen had lowered their income-tax rates. Though politicians on both local and state levels predicted disaster for government services and public education, their forecasts turned out to be wrong. Broder is skeptical about initiatives, however, and does not want them to become a dominant form of lawmaking. To explain why, he shows how money has occasionally influenced the outcomes.

But some of the details he dislikes about the process are technical and can be (and already have been, in some cases) easily addressed. The important point he misses is that nobody expects this particular check on government power to be "perfect." Nothing ever is. The question we should be asking is: What is the alternative?

Over the course of one hundred years, according to Dane Waters, president of the Initiative and Referendum Institute, the U.S. had 1,902 statewide initiatives, of which 787 were adopted. But in 1996–97 alone, the Minnesota legislature (to use just one example) considered 6,656 laws, of which it adopted 422—half as many, in other words, as were accepted by citizens of their own initiative in twenty-four states over one hundred years. Guess which laws got more attention and scrutiny? In 1998, the twenty-four states adopted just thirty-five laws using the initiative process. During that same year, the same states adopted fourteen thousand laws, after considering more than seventy thousand. The abuse of power this represents (it's like a full employment act for lawyers, accountants, lobbyists, and bureaucrats) could have been prevented if the initiative process was part of the constitution, an inalienable right to direct statutory lawmaking procedures. The initiative process has its flaws, certainly. But the passing of fourteen thousand new laws—and the resulting legal, fiscal, and regulatory complexity—gives added power to politicians because they are the ones who know how to navigate the maze and find the loopholes.

Critics worry that direct democracy could lead to the rule of mobs and threaten individual and human rights. But such concerns are unfounded: it has not happened in places where the system has been properly practiced. Moreover, what danger there is to human rights can be eliminated by restricting the range of subjects on which initiatives and plebiscites can be held—as is the case in Switzerland.

The United States today is a good example of how this process evolves from the bottom up, not the top down. In addition to the fiscal issues discussed above, initiatives there have covered quite a range. In 1992, for example, voters in different parts of the country responded to sixty-nine ballot initiatives—more than at any other time since 1932. Voters in Colorado refused to approve special rights for homosexuals in a November referendum, but that same year, Oregonians rejected a measure to declare homosexuality "wrong, unnatural and perverse." On June 2, 1992, a non-binding referendum on the division of California into two states appeared on the ballots. It was approved by 55 percent of the voters; in twenty-seven of thirty-one counties, the proposal gained a majority. In fact, in California any issue can now be put to a statewide vote if 615,958 signatures are collected. In 1996, voters there passed both Proposition 218 (which requires voter approval for increases in local taxes) and Proposition 210 (which increased state minimum wages), and defeated Proposition 217 (which would have increased the top income-tax rates). Californians also passed Proposition 209, abolishing affirmative action, and Proposition 215, legalizing the medical use of marijuana (though the state attorney general challenged it).

Animal-rights groups stopped cock-fighting in Arizona and Missouri, protected horses from butchers in California, and saved bears from baiters in Missouri. In Alaska, an initiative banned billboards. Voters in the state of Washington approved a measure to index minimum wages, and another to end racial preferences in government hiring and contracting. (The last case belies Broder's fears about initiatives being dominated by big money; Boeing and Microsoft were both in favor of maintaining racial preferences, but the campaign they financed was defeated.)

In Arizona, meanwhile, a 1996 initiative legalized marijuana for medical purposes. The legislature undid it. Then, in 1998, Arizonans passed a measure to prevent both the legislature and the governor from undoing future referenda. In Mississippi, Missouri, and Wyoming, however, voters backed measures that made it harder to put initiatives on the ballot.

Perhaps the most serious objection to referenda and initiatives, however, will come from politicians, lawyers, accountants—all the people who benefit from the complexity and lack of transparency that the passing of fourteen thousand obscure laws a year allows.

Referenda and initiatives also strike a blow against lobbyists and their dependence on political maneuvering. They deprive politicians of their role as favor-brokers, because they can never be sure what they will be allowed to do in office or how long they will be allowed to stay there. There is also less money in pork barrels, since taxpayers have the option of voting on every project proposed by their governments. Such changes can also be expected to weaken adherence to—and thus blur—party lines, since referenda diminish incentives to form inflexible alliances. We should not be surprised, therefore, that few politicians—or political parties—are advocating institutional changes that would permanently curtail their own power.

SIGNS OF THE FUTURE:
THE PROSPECTS FOR DIRECT DEMOCRACY

Nevertheless, one of the significant political changes of the final decade of the twentieth century was that many important decisions in various parts of the world—and not only in the United States— were decided by referenda. In March 1992, white South Africans voted for reform. Later that same year, Danes defeated the European Community's Maastricht Treaty while the French approved it. In October 1992, Canadians overwhelmingly vetoed a wishy-washy, mishmash document that politicians tried to pass off as significant constitutional reform. And in 2000, Danes decided to stick with their own currency rather than adopting the tumbling Euro.

In June 1991, 96 percent of the Italians who went to the polls voted yes in a referendum designed to reduce corruption in elections. The referendum was initiated by Mario Segni, a dissident Christian-Democrat, and was opposed by the leaders of the big parties. On April 11, 1993, President Boris Yeltsin of Russia held a referendum to allow Russians to decide on the allocation of powers between president and Parliament.

Of course, the mere fact that these referenda took place does not mean that politicians suddenly favor giving citizens more power. People have always wanted greater control over their political institutions. As early as 1913, 3,982 Canadians answered yes to the following question: "Are you in favor of having the Initiative, Referendum and Right of Recall placed upon the Statute of Books of your own province?" Only sixty-two people voted no. Yet in spite of such overwhelming support, the institutions were not introduced.

So why the shift since 1992? One explanation is that politicians have decided to rely on referenda not because they want to see them become a permanent institution, but because they hope to win approval for their bold departures and embarrass the opposition (and gain more power, in Yeltsin's case). Politicians also sometimes use referenda to evade responsibility for a difficult decision. (In Ireland, for example, the abortion issue was decided in a referendum.)

But there is a more fundamental explanation. As we saw earlier, governments suddenly ceased relying on referenda during the Great Depression, a time when governments in both the United States and Europe had inadvertently destroyed their capital markets and were struggling with the severe consequences of unemployment. Then came the Second World War and the Cold War, neither of which provided the right timing to experiment with new political institutions. Priorities were elsewhere.

But this is exactly a reason to be cautiously optimistic about the current possibility of significant changes in political institutions. Such changes may happen even though politicians do not want them—either because the coffers of governments around the world are empty, or because their ability to tax diminished significantly during the past ten years (when capital, both financial and human, was able to move with greater ease). Historical evidence from all fields of human activity—science, technology, political affairs, and so on—suggests that radical innovations were rarely carried out when the establishment had access to finance.

When it has such access, it can sustain armies, police forces, and myth-industries to keep itself in power. But as Joseph Schumpeter understood, when coffers are empty, existing political institutions crumble. It happened in England a number of times, as well as in France, Japan, and, more recently, Russia. In a less dramatic way, it is happening now in Mexico, and in 1997–98 it happened all over Asia.

As long as governments can tax or have access to credit, no information technology, no humanitarian efforts from abroad, and not even the senility of their leaders can topple them (how long did the Russian geriatrics rule?). Once governments do not have the money, however, it becomes a different story. Then comes the rumbling, the grumbling, the discontent and pessimism because of declining standards of living—even among those most dedicated, on the surface, to the bankrupt government's ideology. That's when the political edifice crumbles.

The historical evidence suggests that government cash flow and credit problems lead to significant political changes only when people despair of the system and no longer see the fiscal problems as consequences of wars, accidents, or corruption. This is, in fact, the definition of the term "fiscal crisis." Indeed, in a recent article, "The Coming Clash of Welfare States," Irving Kristol argues that "people who have been told that they are entitled to a welfare state—and are not told that they cannot afford it—. . . rebel against any effort to limit the expenditures. An underdeveloped country with a welfare state is a recipe for authoritarian government, because only an authoritarian regime can control both the people and the government. . . . They will never create viable democracies." This conclusion may be too pessimistic. Another option, as we saw in previous chapters, is to open up capital markets while diminishing spending.

Countries where the idea of accountability has stronger roots may take the institutions of direct democracy down from the shelves. When combined with a continuous move toward the democratization of capital markets, this makes a winning combination. The technology needed to bring this political system to life is now available at low cost. And it is happening—from the bottom up. *Pace* Machiavelli—whose prince never arrived—the trends summarized in this chapter suggest that the "wisdom of many" will help the spread of these institutions. Let princes belong to fairy tales—and to societies that kept their capital markets closed. These societies need the kiss of the handsome prince to wake them from either their somnolence or cycles of violence to create institutions that will bring hope and prosperity.

CHAPTER 5

MONETARY STANDARDS AND THE INTERNATIONAL FINANCIAL SYSTEM

Stable money is necessary for the development of open capital markets. Yet many governments have failed to stabilize their currencies, sometimes on purpose and at other times inadvertently. The latter happens with governments that choose to pursue a variety of faddish policies that draw on macroeconomic theory, which is based on a misunderstanding of what money is. Whether such destabilization is inadvertent or not, however, one consequence is the lack of development of vibrant capital markets. Clearly, the sooner we get rid of today's fads, the more quickly our economic problems will be resolved.

This chapter is a reminder that "money" is a matter of trust, and that it fulfills its roles best when people view it as a standard for pricing all contractual agreements. The only role of the central banks should be to sustain this standard. When monetary policy is guided by other objectives, the results vary from disastrous to painful. Once this point of view is accepted, we will have overcome one obstacle in the path toward democratizing our capital markets.

In 1997, when Asian tigers turned into pussycats seemingly overnight—with Thailand, the Philippines, Indonesia, and Malaysia watching their stock markets tumble and their currencies sink by 25 to 85 percent—Alan Greenspan, the chairman of the Federal Reserve Board, and Robert Rubin, the then treasury secretary, began giving speeches and testimonies emphasizing the need for currency stability as a precondition for prosperity. But an issue that neither Greenspan nor Rubin addressed was this: Currency stability relative to what?

During the first nine months of 1998, the American dollar appreciated relative to all other currencies and commodity prices. But was it "stable"? How do we know if something is stable if we do not have a speed-of-light benchmark against which to measure it? Some argue that anchoring monetary policies in domestic price indices, such as the consumer price index (CPI), will bring about such stability. Not so.

Although Japan, the U.S., Canada, and Germany have all achieved a relatively high degree of domestic price stability since 1998, the U.S. dollar/yen, the U.S. dollar/Deutschmark, and the U.S. dollar/Canadian dollar exchange rates have continued to be volatile (as has the U.S. dollar/Euro rate since its inception). During the past ten years, the measured inflation rate in these countries was low, yet exchange rates changed by 50 percent or more. And since its inception in January 1999, the Euro has depreciated by roughly 25 percent relative to the U.S. dollar, in spite of the fact that the European countries and the U.S. have had (and, according to interest rate differentials, are expected to continue to have) comparable inflation rates. These currencies were not "stable." How does one explain these fluctuations? This chapter will answer that question too.

While Greenspan and Rubin were advocating currency stability, the IMF and members of the economic profession were occasional propagators of devaluation and floating exchange rates. Politicians and some economists, in Europe as well as Canada (countries with tumbling currencies), have argued either that the decline is beneficial for their countries or that financial markets do not know what they are doing (that is, that the currencies are "undervalued," and that this undervaluation has nothing to do with the "fundamentals"). They blamed "irrational financial markets" and speculators for the declining currencies (though they are the first to claim credit when the currencies rise).

Yet the facts are that both Canada and the European countries saw personal incomes stagnate and their stock markets—which reflect expectations of future wealth creation—underperform those in the United States. In Mexico too, in 1997, three years after the curiously still praised December 1994 devaluation, the stock market stood at 40 percent of its pre-devaluation value in terms of the U.S. dollar, and the inflation rate remained in the double digits. All this, then, raises an additional question: Since depreciating currencies have often been accompanied by inflation, higher nominal interest rates, and expectations of less wealth creation, why do economists and politicians still defend this policy? This chapter will deal with this question too.

Now that Asian markets have partially rebounded, what are we to make of theories that attributed the fall of the Asian currencies to cronyism, to lack of transparency, to political decisions regarding the allocation of capital? After all, none of these circumstances has changed significantly in the few years since the 1997 crisis. Clearly, something other than allocating capital based on cronyism and the rule of kleptocrats provoked the crisis. That "something other" had to do with both mismanaged currencies and the role the IMF has played.

This chapter will thus also look into the following questions:

- What is the origin of the idea that currency depreciation is a solution for countries that wish to increase or restore their competitiveness, cut their current-account deficits, and build up foreign reserves?
- What alternative policies can be used to help solve those problems that policy-makers and economists tried to solve by debasing currencies?
- How did the IMF contribute—inadvertently, perhaps—to currency crises?

First, though, we must look into the meaning of the term "currency stability" and answer this question: Stability relative to what?

SEPARATING MONEY FROM POLITICS

As we saw briefly in chapter one, there are four options for separating monetary policy from politics. Each one is also supposed to anchor monetary policy, preventing inflation and deflation. The four options are:

1. monetary rule;
2. currency boards;
3. inflationary targets; and
4. adopting the gold standard.

And there is another option: to abolish the monopoly national governments have on issuing currencies, and let free banking thrive. That, however, would involve such drastic changes that discussing it at this stage would be impractical.

In a September 5, 1997, speech at Stanford University, Alan Greenspan addressed the aforementioned options, starting with the following observation: "Whatever its successes, the current monetary policy regime is far from ideal. Each episode has had to be treated as unique or nearly so. It may have been the best we could do at the moment. But we continuously examine alternatives that might better anchor policy, so that it becomes less subject to the abilities of the Federal Open Market Committee to analyze developments and make predictions."

The first option Greenspan tackled in his speech was Milton Friedman's well-known recommendation for expanding the money supply at a constant rate. Greenspan dismissed this as an option for anchoring monetary policy because its success in preventing inflation and deflation has been proven to depend on the stable velocity of an agreed-upon definition of the term "money supply." (The word "velocity," in this sense, refers to how often the thus defined "money" changes hands, on average, during a set period of time.) Greenspan stated that over the past decade, he had not found either stable velocity or definitions for "money" that could serve him in designing policies. He did not rule out the possibility of periods of stable velocity, however, in which case a monetary rule could guide policy.

Greenspan's observation was not surprising, even for those who share the belief that inflation is always a monetary phenomenon. When 170 central banks mismanage their currencies, and there are drastic changes in fiscal policies, the domestic and international demands for currencies fluctuate, and the velocity of a currency does not stay stable. This is exactly the set of circumstances we've seen during the past few decades. When global investors expect the Federal Reserve Board to manage the U.S. dollar better than other central banks manage their own currencies, their demand for the dollar increases and that for other currencies drops.

The resulting increase in the value of the dollar relative to other currencies depends on—among other things—what the Federal Reserve Board and other central banks do. If the board does not accommodate such demand, and the other central banks do not absorb the unwanted liquidity in their own currencies, then, in our world of floating exchange rates, the dollar will rise far more than it would if the board pursued a more accommodating policy. In both cases, however, velocity of both the U.S. dollar and all other currencies would change.

Greenspan then mentioned a currently popular academic theory (a variation on the inflationary target idea), the so-called Taylor rule, which suggests that monetary policy can be guided by looking at prices and measures of output. He dismisses this recommendation, too, on the grounds that, for this theory to work, economists and politicians must first know some key features of the economy, and these key features must be stable. But he was unable to uncover such features.

One alternative that Greenspan did not discuss in his speech is the establishment of a currency board. Since he was addressing only monetary policy in the U.S., his avoidance of this option is understandable.

A currency board links a domestic currency to a foreign one at a fixed rate. Such a board makes monetary policy independent of *domestic* politics, and this has been a successful means of preventing inflation. Hong Kong and Argentina are among the countries that have adopted currency boards, linking their currencies to the U.S. dollar. This arrangement poses problems, however, if the foreign central bank (the bank in the country to whose currency the local one is linked) makes mistakes or pursues a domestic political goal of its own.

Another way to achieve the separation of monetary policy from politics is to target inflation rates, keeping them below a certain level. But changes in the CPI, the most frequently chosen target, have often turned out to be political after all. (We will explore this further in the discussion of the choice of a harmonized CPI in the European Community.) Moreover, there have been many technical problems with price indices. These have in turn led central banks into mazes of error, and to volatile exchange rates. Let us take a closer look at why this apparently technical, seemingly non-political guide for monetary policy can have a destabilizing effect on currency values. Once this issue is made clear, we will examine how the last option left, a variation on fixed exchange rates and the gold price standard, provides a non-political anchor for guiding monetary policy, and also brings about both price and currency stability.

CPI TARGETS AND CURRENCY INSTABILITY

Let's consider first the New Zealand experiment of the early 1990s. That country's CPI was heavily weighted in the property sector when prices in that sector were suddenly driven up by a surge of East Asian capital flows. As the result of an agreement between the finance minister and the governor of the central bank, the Reserve Bank of New Zealand had a mandate to keep inflation below 2 percent. The government had the right to change the target, but only after explaining any desired change to both Parliament and the public. If the bank's governor failed to comply with the government-mandated target, he could be fired before his term expired.

In response to the surge in capital inflows, the aforementioned regulations, and a price index that overestimated the "true" level of inflation, however, the Reserve Bank of New Zealand tightened its monetary policy. This resulted in further capital inflows, a strengthened currency, and a weak GDP growth. Subsequently, the government and the bank raised the inflation target to 3 percent. Later, the bank's governor declared that he would no longer target a specific price index, but would address the "underlying inflation." However, when he was asked how this level of inflation would be calculated, the governor was evasive.

A similar sequence of events took place in Canada during the early 1990s. Although the federal government imposed a 7 percent sales tax (and the provincial government in Quebec another 8 percent on top of it), which led to an increase in the (mis)measured CPI, the central bank targeted zero percent inflation—as measured by the CPI. The result—as in New Zealand—was a tight monetary policy (the money supply dropped by more than 5 percent during 1990), increased interest rates, a stronger Canadian dollar, capital inflows, diminished exports, and recession. In 1992, after more than two years of this misguided monetary experiment, the Bank of Canada revised its policy, and the Canadian dollar dropped from a high of ninety cents (measured against the U.S. dollar) to a low of seventy-seven cents.

These examples show how misinterpreted and miscalculated price indices can lead to mistaken monetary policies and fluctuations in currencies. Thus a country could have domestic "price stability"—as mismeasured by conventional price indices—and a fluctuating currency at the same time.

Consider now events in Japan since 1986. Between 1986 and the end of 1989, that country's central bank pursued a lax monetary policy. Yet neither the CPI nor the wholesale price index reflected the laxity. The CPI increased by 0.6 percent in 1986, 0.1 percent in 1987, and 0.7 percent in 1988, before jumping to 2.3 percent and 3.1 percent in 1989 and 1990, respectively. But the wholesale price index was at the same level in 1990 that it had been in 1986. Did the Bank of Japan continue to pursue a lax monetary policy because it misread these price indices? Maybe. Why wasn't the sharp increase in real-estate values reflected in price indices?

Sixty percent of Japanese own their own homes, and a large percentage live in company-subsidized or public housing. The number of merged households (those with two or more adult generations living together) is 50 percent in Japan, but stands at only 2 to 3 percent in the U.S. and the U.K. and 9 percent in France. I could not find out how the Japanese Statistical Bureau calculates the price of housing and its weight in its indices under these circumstances. But by putting this information together with the fact that during the real-estate boom years the Japanese price indices barely moved, we can conclude that at 20 percent the housing component in Japanese price indices was underestimated. The fact that younger generations could not afford to rent or own their own dwellings was not visible.

Nevertheless, the lax monetary policy led to inflationary expectations—even if official indices did not capture them. So what did the Japanese do? They invested in real estate and in equities (in Japan, more so than in the U.S., equities were backed by real estate), pushing up stock prices. The Japanese government then compounded the monetary mistake by committing a series of fiscal mistakes. Beginning in 1988, it imposed a 20 percent withholding tax on personal savings, a capital gains tax on equity sales, a securities transfer tax, a 3 percent consumption tax, a 6 percent tax on new cars, and a 2.5 percent surtax on corporate profits. On top of it all, it drastically increased capital gains taxes on real estate in 1990. Before then, a 17 percent capital gains tax came into effect after five years. But starting in 1990, this low tax came into effect only after ten years. To avoid the 57 percent tax on real estate, owners had to hold on to their properties for five years or more. In 1990, this was extended to ten years. The consequences were as expected: a large drop in the value of real-estate equities, diminished growth, and diminished demand for yen liquidity.

At the end of 1989, the Bank of Japan tightened its monetary policy. But more than a decade later, Japan still lives with the consequences of this series of monetary and fiscal policies. This additional example shows why the combination of stable domestic price indices and fluctuating currency values is not such a puzzle after all. In a world of floating exchange rates and rapid capital flows, large currency fluctuations can be caused—even when mismeasured price indices stay stable—by a mix of drastic changes in fiscal policies and the tightening or relaxing of monetary policy in response to mismeasured inflation rates.

The Japanese experience should have raised red flags among Euro optimists. Let us forget for the moment that we cannot yet anticipate the politics surrounding this currency, and that the flagrant manipulation of deficit and debt numbers before the Euro's introduction was hardly wise if one wanted to establish trust in this currency. Instead, there are other issues that should have been of concern.

Much has been made of the fact that the goal of the European Central Bank (ECB) is "price stability," for example. But the price index the bank chose is a "harmonized" one that does not include health care, education, or the cost of owner-occupied housing. That the European countries expected to be guided by such an index did not bode well for the future of their monetary policy and the value of the Euro. The situation has been exacerbated by the fact that the United States has been moving toward lower taxes, while Europe has stayed frozen in high-tax/high-regulatory mode (contrary to the expectations that preceded the introduction of the Euro). The ECB did not react to the resulting capital outflows, nor did it absorb the unwanted Euro liquidity. And when Europeans began exchanging their many disparate currencies for one common currency, they created even more unwanted liquidity with the Euro. Since the ECB did not absorb this excess liquidity, as Robert Mundell (the 1999 Nobel Prize winner in economics) pointed out, the decline in the Euro should have been expected.

What can we conclude from all of the above? In a world of floating exchange rates, when countries pursue drastic changes in fiscal and regulatory policies, currencies will fluctuate—even if central banks keep domestic price stability. In principle, targeting price indices will separate monetary policy from politics, but in practice it does not. The reaction of the central banks to mismeasured (or poorly chosen) price indices can have costly consequences, which voters then ask to be corrected through the political process.

HOW ABOUT GOLD AND FIXED EXCHANGE RATES?

Neither the monetary growth rule nor an inflationary target ensures, then, stability in the value of a currency. And currency boards still mean dependence on another central bank's policy. So what option is left to those who wish to bring about a stable price level and stable currencies, while at the same time separating monetary policy from politics (which should be the fundamentals of the much-touted new global financial architecture)? The answer—as paradoxical as this may sound in a digital age—is to go back to fixed exchange rates anchored in the gold price.

Gold price?! With the exception of the aforementioned Robert Mundell, Jude Wanniski (who, together with Mundell and Arthur Laffer, was the father of supply-side economics), the *Wall Street Journal, Forbes* magazine, and Alan Greenspan himself, few experts have argued for using changes in the price of gold to anchor monetary policy. Before becoming chairman of the Federal Reserve Board, Greenspan was an ardent advocate of the gold standard, as his article in *Capitalism: The Unknown Ideal,* a book honoring the novelist Ayn Rand, shows. And in his September 5, 1997, speech at Stanford University, Greenspan still had this to say about gold: "Gold was such an anchor or rule prior to World War I, but it was first compromised and eventually abandoned because it restrained the type of discretionary monetary and fiscal policies that modern democracies appear to value." Notice his typically careful wording. Greenspan did not say that these discretionary policies *have value* as far as prosperity is concerned—just that they *appear* to *be valued.*

Let us see, then, how this anchor guides monetary policy, and how the stock-market turbulence often experienced during currency crises can be linked to the absence of such a monetary standard. Remember, though, that fixing currencies (and linking them all to such a standard) has nothing to do with gold coins, or with gold being a hedge against inflation. Instead, establishing a non-political, market-based standard means anchoring prices and contracts and providing central bankers with signals about changes in demands for liquidity.

Anchoring Prices and Contracts

Changes in relative prices signal consumers, producers, and investors that it's time to reallocate their resources. But what are these changes "relative" to? Let's say, for example, that there are one thousand commodities and services either currently available or to be delivered in the future. In the absence of a fixed anchor or a common yardstick, there would be 499,500 possible relative prices, as each commodity or service would be priced in relation to every other one. With a common yardstick, however, there would be 999 prices and that's it. This is why societies both large and small have, since time immemorial, agreed on a yardstick, a standard. In ancient Rome, it was salt (that's where the word "salary" comes from); other societies have used pepper, rocks, silver, gold, and (in prisons, for example) cigarettes.

Eventually, through a long process of trial and error, people around the world agreed that gold and silver served well as standards against which everything else—all contracts—could be priced. Once such a standard was chosen, there could be neither inflation nor deflation unless relatively vast amounts of gold or silver were either discovered or destroyed. Indeed, for the roughly two hundred years that England used such standards (with few interruptions), the wholesale price index remained more or less constant. It was roughly one hundred in 1717, for example, when Sir Isaac Newton linked the pound sterling to gold, and it was still about one hundred in 1930. This constancy was achieved not because the monetary authorities used this index to guide monetary policy, but because the index was a result of linking the pound to gold. It's significant too that this price stability was maintained even though England went through dramatic technological changes during those two centuries (much as we are going through today).

113

As long as private and central banks linked their paper currency to either gold or silver, and as long as people believed that the arrangement was stable, it did not matter whether contractual agreements to buy present and future commodities and services were priced in terms of gold or the paper currency. It does make a difference, however, if both gold and silver are used as standards; their prices fluctuate in relation to each other. But if contracts are priced against currencies linked at times to silver and at other times to gold, then there is an incentive to create an additional market to arbitrage; this would allow companies to insure against fluctuations between these two standards.

In practice, linking paper currencies to the two standards brought about financial crises when governments interfered and fixed the price of silver in terms of gold. Though the next sequence of events happened about one hundred years ago in the United States—*the* emerging country of those times—it shows the chaos that ensues when governments get into the business of pricing currencies (chaos that is strikingly similar to what we saw in the wake of the 1997 Asian currency crises).

Grover Cleveland was just starting his second term as president in 1893 when he gave rise to expectations that he was about to repeal the law requiring the U.S. to back its bonds with gold. He also wanted to break the artificial link between the value of an ounce of gold and the value of a silver coin—a link that grew out of the ill-conceived Sherman Silver Purchase Act of 1890—at a time when most transactions were conducted in silver.

The effects were immediate. Once exuberant European investors pulled out of the U.S., credit collapsed, unemployment increased to 20 percent, silver mines in the West closed, riots broke out, and the people marched on Washington. In several speeches, President Cleveland insisted that the country's fundamentals were sound, though to no avail. He then turned to John Pierpont Morgan and August Belmont, the two great financiers of the time, and suggested they form a syndicate to market bonds for gold in Europe. They succeeded where politicians could not. In 1900,

Congress passed the Gold Standard Act, which put the country on a pure gold standard, ending the practice of relying on two metals as standards. (Note, however, that the upheaval happened not because there were two metallic standards, but because the government arbitrarily fixed the price of one of them.)

If the prices of these two metals were not fixed by decree, the problems associated with linking them with paper currencies would be easy to solve today, especially compared with the costs of solving the problems of 170 mainly mismanaged paper currencies anchored solely in the vague promises and politics of the world's central bankers. The latter gave rise to many unique financial instruments in new "derivative" markets, which are designed to insure against currency fluctuations. Businesses trading across borders hedge, freeing themselves to focus on their corporate activities rather than being drawn into the foreign-exchange business. But for global businesses, the cost of insuring against dozens of fluctuating currencies does not come cheap. If prices were linked to just two metallic standards, the derivative markets would be significantly reduced in scope.

What this all tells us is that fluctuating currencies impose costs on international trade. These costs were neither as significant nor as obvious in the past, when most countries around the world had severe barriers against trade and capital, both financial and human, was less mobile.

FIXED EXCHANGE RATES LINKED TO A METALLIC STANDARD

How does the monetary system work when currencies are linked to a metallic standard? Well, in this kind of system, central bankers do not have to guess growth, understand and estimate velocity, or be able to forecast what will happen to millions of variables in domestic and international economies. When people show up at the bank and want to exchange currency for gold, it's done, diminishing liquidity. The bank reacts when the price of gold goes up or down by, say, 3 percent relative to a fixed target price. If the price increases by 3 percent, the central bank absorbs liquidity by either selling gold or issuing bonds. And if it drops by 3 percent, the bank buys back gold or bonds, injecting liquidity. The gold price acts as a signal of what is happening to liquidity in the economy; there's no need to have statisticians, economists, and central bankers gathering, massaging, and interpreting price indices.

The economist Stanley Jevons called this the "gold par method," and he describes it this way in his 1903 book *Money and the Mechanism of Exchange*:

> Assuming an inconvertible paper currency to be issued, and to be entirely in the hands of government, many evils of such a system might be avoided if the issue were limited or reduced the moment that the price of gold in paper rose above par. As long as the notes and the gold coins, which they pretend to represent, circulate on a footing of equality, they are as good as convertible. Since the beginning of the Franco-Prussian war, the Bank of France appears to have acted successfully on this principle, and the inconvertible notes were never depreciated more than about ½ or 1 percent in spite of the vast political and financial troubles in France.

This mechanism has absolutely nothing in common with popular views of gold as a store of value or a hedge against inflation. The price of gold simply anchors prices, currencies, and monetary policy. It is a benchmark against which—implicitly—everything else is priced, and which by definition does not allow either inflation or deflation to happen (unless significant amounts of gold are suddenly either destroyed or discovered). The goal of the central bank then becomes to maintain this standard, thus anchoring contracts, which are the basis of a commercial society. Nothing is perfect, of course, and the central bank's short-term tolerance to a 3 percent fluctuation in the price of gold means that temporary variations in purchasing power are not entirely eliminated.

How can gold reserves be defended? As we saw earlier, central banks must do this by issuing bonds in the local currency and draining the surplus liquidity from the banking system. This option also exists today as a barrier against inflation, but central banks do not have to exercise it. For example, in Mexico in 1994, the government, after secretly inundating the economy with unwanted pesos (for political reasons), opted for devaluation and inflation. Mexico's central bank avoided the option of absorbing the unwanted peso liquidity. Once a currency is anchored in gold, however, a central bank cannot pursue such an option without destroying its own credibility, and that of the country's government.

Misinterpreted History

If this is so simple, why then, you may now be asking, did the world abandon the gold standard, and eventually fixed exchange rates? It is important to answer this question, because if we can conclude that this shift was based on a misinterpretation of events, it would be easier and more efficient to revamp the system by simply "unlearning" the present practices.

Let us first examine the problems the U.K. faced between 1925 and 1931, years that saw a decline in the belief in the effectiveness of the gold standard, and the rise of the idea that central bankers and economists would be better off designing new policies to bring about prosperity than adjusting old policies in response to market signals. In 1925, while serving as chancellor of the exchequer under Prime Minister Stanley Baldwin, Winston Churchill made the mistake of restoring the depreciated English pound (which had depreciated when the U.K. suspended the gold standard during the First World War) to its pre-war gold value. This mistaken political decision suddenly increased the value of the pound, raising arbitrarily the price of everything denominated in its terms (relative to other countries' prices). To avoid such arbitrary appreciation, every contractual agreement—including employment contracts—would have had to have been adjusted downward. That did not happen.

Economists of the time (Friedrich Hayek was an exception) misinterpreted the sequence of events, and attributed the problems not

117

to the political decision to re-link the pound to gold at the wrong rate, but rather to wages being too rigid to be adjusted quickly. Their solution—and Keynes was a proponent of this—was to pursue an inflationary policy to quickly diminish wages. But this solution is not feasible under a gold standard, as we saw earlier. Eventually, in September 1931, Britain abandoned the standard altogether.

Other earlier political interventions signaled that governments possibly misunderstood the discipline that adhering to the gold standard requires, or else they were no longer committed to maintaining such discipline. Some economists still point to a sequence of events that took place between 1929 and 1931 in Austria as proof that adhering to the standard fails to prevent financial crises. In truth, these events prove that the problem is elsewhere: in using monetary policy for political purposes. Once monetary policy is guided by something other than the need to maintain the stability of the currency, the gold standard cannot be sustained. Here is how Anna Schwartz (who co-authored, with Milton Friedman, several classic studies of monetary theory) describes the Austrian events in a 1998 speech:

> Brad DeLong cites the case of the collapse of the Austrian Credit-Anstalt in 1931 as proof of private-sector failure to prevent financial crisis. The facts refute DeLong. The Credit-Anstalt was Austria's largest deposit bank. Its financial condition had worsened since 1929. In May 1931 the bank's losses for the preceding year, which wiped out its official capital, became known. The Austrian government then injected capital funds into the bank. Suspicion that the bank's losses were greater than disclosed led to large-scale withdrawals by domestic and foreign depositors. Capital flight followed. Foreign credits obtained by Austria's central bank were accompanied by the agreement by foreign banks not to withdraw deposits. The internal drain continued, whereupon the government adopted exchange controls rather than openly abandoning the gold parity of the Austrian schilling.

A monetary standard cannot be sustained when governments inject capital into banks for political reasons, when central bankers fail in their role as lenders of last resort, and when banks adopt exchange controls. Such mistakes discredited the gold standard, and led economists to invent falsely imagined pasts. The problems were not with the standard itself, however. Schwartz goes on to say:

> The Credit-Anstalt was insolvent. No lender was ready to rescue it. If Austria had shut it, withdrawals would have ended. Austria could then have negotiated a settlement with the bank's creditors. The argument that it takes time to arrange a settlement is not compelling. That is the nature of the sequel to default. The Credit-Anstalt debacle was the prelude to Britain's helping itself by abandoning the gold standard in September 1931. Reflation and recovery from the Depression then became possible. In 1931, if the Federal Reserve was not ready to act as a lender of last resort, the U.S. could also have abandoned the gold standard at that juncture and saved the country eighteen further months of severe contraction. DeLong's contention that the policies of the 1930s were private-sector failures at best is questionable.

How can people calculate prices and enter into long-term contractual agreements when currencies are no longer anchored? In his aforementioned September speech, Alan Greenspan alludes to the link between currency values and pricing long-term contractual agreements. He notes that "as long as individuals make contractual agreements for future payments valued in dollars and other currencies, there must be a presumption on the part of those involved in the transaction about the future purchasing power of money. . . . Hence we must assume that embodied in all products is some unit of output, and hence of price, that is recognizable to producers and consumers and upon which they will base their decision." Greenspan dismisses the possibility of using price indices and inflation-indexed bonds as a substitute, but he does not mention what the standard should then be. As chairman of the Federal Reserve Board, Greenspan must be circumspect. Reverting to fixed exchange rates with gold as an anchor would change the rules of political games around the world.

In a lecture titled "An Economic Interpretation of Our Time," delivered at the Lowell Institute in Boston back in 1941, Joseph Schumpeter makes this point effectively. He states: "Gold is not popular because it ruthlessly and tactlessly always tells the truth." Once currencies are stable, the flow of capital—both financial and human—depends on a country's fiscal policies and its ability to attract and retain skilled people. Politicians avoid situations that would so clearly signal their mistaken policies.

But it would be misleading to say today that politicians alone oppose monetary standards. Banks and those specializing in derivatives should not be expected to support such transitions either. A monetary standard is as much a threat to them as a flat tax is to the accounting and legal professions.

DEVALUATIONS AND MONETARY ANCHORS

As the saying goes, there is no smoke without fire. Until now, this chapter has explained the types of mistaken policies that helped discredit the gold standard and establish a world of paper currencies backed by the idea that "money" is a policy tool rather than a trusted unit of account. But what events helped create the theory that debasing currencies was a means of producing prosperity? And how did the idea of floating currencies gain favor? The next sections answer these questions.

The 1950s saw economists praising so-called infant industries and import-substitution strategies as keys to prosperity. The many victims of what were really just faddish academic rationalizations of political interests included India, Brazil and other Latin American nations, and several African countries. Rulers and government leaders in these countries were happy to sponsor and promote these ideas, since they gave scientific legitimacy to their quests for increased power.

But import substitution—that is, barring better and cheaper imports from a country, and producing shoddy domestic substitutes instead—proved to be a costly exercise. Its failure led numerous Asian governments to look for alternative development strategies. What they hoped to achieve was a degree of prosperity, without giving up much political power. Export-driven prosperity was a solution, since it meant they could rely on the policies of other countries, rather than having to carry out drastic internal changes. Selling abroad can cover for political mistakes at home.

And although consumers can benefit as much from importers as they do from exporters, it makes political sense to favor exporters. Importers and traders, whose business is to scout the globe for the best combination of goods, services, prices, and quality, can transfer their skills to other parts of the world with greater ease. As a result, they offer less political support than export businesses, whose plants are wedded to territory. Politicians—the most immobile of all professionals—know that they can depend on other immobile groups. It's little wonder that since time immemorial, governments have bestowed prizes and honors on exporters, and none on importers or traders—not to mention financiers.

Japan and several other Asian countries adopted this "export growth" model, taxing their citizens to subsidize export industries and boost sales to overseas customers. The strategy worked for a while because the prospering Western democracies bought the subsidized goods. The Asian countries accumulated formidable reserves, had high savings and low unemployment, and saw their currencies appreciate as demand for their exports grew. Superficial theories and statistical correlations helped establish the myth of export-led growth as a credible universal strategy for strengthening currencies, and this became a politically "desirable" (desirable for an elite, that is) alternative model to the U.S.-type economy, where capital markets are more open and the government's role more limited.

The mistaken lesson many economists drew from Asia's success was that if governments first devalue their currencies, they then can export themselves to prosperity, accumulate foreign reserves, and employ more people. Why has this approach now failed so visibly in Asia? And how is it that for years most Western observers misjudged the solidity of these export-driven economies?

Societies are judged by their "prosperity." For years, prosperity was confused with rates of savings, levels of employment, investments, current accounts, or short-term growth as measured by GNP or GDP numbers—numbers that pay absolutely no attention to the matching process emphasized in previous chapters, and that are often (mis)measured in terms of depreciating currencies. Thus the suggestion that the Asian model of development is a "general" one, and that it provides a comprehensive recipe for prosperity, is wrong. It is wrong not only because these policies do not bring lasting prosperity, but also because the temporary prosperity they occasionally bring depends both on the consumption demands of countries with more open capital markets and on few governments around the world emulating the model. Let's look now at how the IMF has added to the confusion and contributed to currency volatility.

HOW THE IMF DISTORTS

In the early 1990s, Mexico had a fixed exchange rate of 3.1 pesos to the U.S. dollar. As the 1994 elections drew close, the central bank did what it has done in every election year for decades: it printed money—secretly. When Mexican investors got hold of this information, they withdrew roughly $20–25 billion from Mexico. Foreign investors followed suit. Although the central bank could have restored credibility by issuing bonds and buying back the unwanted pesos, it chose not to. In December, the peso began a dramatic decline, spurred on by the public's justified loss of confidence in the country's monetary policy. The slide continued for three months, with Mexican and IMF authorities debating possible solutions. After a deepening of the crisis in early March 1995, the IMF administered a U.S.-backed $52-billion bailout.

The bailout had a long-term impact on global capital markets and currencies, primarily because such bailouts came to be viewed as official IMF policy. Indeed, the IMF itself encouraged such beliefs, eventually announcing that it intended to act as a lender of last resort in the next financial crisis, and that it needed more funds to play this role.

One result of these events was that from 1995 to 1997, the spread between the bonds of developed countries and those of emerging ones narrowed significantly. Since investors now expected the bonds of emerging countries to be backed by the U.S. treasury, there was no need to pay a risk-premium.

These expectations started to unravel when it became clear that the IMF was not going to bail out everyone after all; they were eliminated entirely when the IMF and the U.S. treasury allowed Russia to default in 1998. As a result, all emerging countries, from Latin America to Asia, have since faced higher interest rates, a reflection of the greater likelihood of their devaluating or defaulting on their bonds. But between 1995 and 1998, the altered expectations increased the volatility of currencies, aggravating problems rather than solving them.

CONCLUSIONS

A trio of insightful observers, George Schultz, William Simon, and Walter Wriston, wrote in a 1998 *Wall Street Journal* article that "the gold standard has been replaced by the information standard, an iron discipline that no government can evade. Foreign exchanges are now set by tens of thousands of traders at computer terminals around the globe. Their judgments about monetary and economic policies are instantly translated in the cross rates of currencies. No country can hide." This is a nice statement. But how do you sign a business contract in the "information standard"? How do you price it?

It's time for us to start rebuilding the much-discussed "global financial infrastructure," and to do that we first have to address the questions raised in this chapter. We now have some of the answers. Let's recap and see what they imply.

For employees, as for businesses, money serves one purpose and one purpose only: it's a basis for contractual agreements. People enter into such agreements to make future payments. These payments must be valued in terms of "something," and there must be a presumption on the part of those involved in the transaction that this "something" will keep its purchasing power during the time horizon fixed in the agreement. If it does not, chaos occasionally ensues, and monetary affairs become complex and impose heavy burdens on commerce, as this chapter showed.

Informal dollarization (that is, people using the U.S. dollar instead of their local paper currencies both in transactions and as basis for their contracts), pegged and floating exchange rates, currency boards—all have been awkward attempts to solve problems that have been created by the absence of a monetary standard and monetary discipline, and the intermingling of monetary affairs and politics. The IMF has only added to the confusion. Nowhere is the misunderstanding of monetary affairs and of recent crises more flagrantly on display than in *The Return of Depression Economics,* the latest book by the *New York Times* columnist Paul Krugman, also of MIT.

The book pretends to provide insights into the financial crises of the late 1990s, the same subjects covered in this chapter. Let's contrast his analysis and recommendations with the ones presented here. Krugman thinks that overvalued currencies and random, self-fulfilling panics brought about the crises. His "solutions" are lasting inflation (in the 3 to 4 percent range), devaluation, tariffs, and capital controls. He believes that people's capricious, unprovoked behavior is the problem. Wise politicians, and presumably even wiser economists, know how to compensate for the unpredictable mood swings of the masses, and they also know how to price currencies.

Krugman starts his book summarizing a wonderful little article, published in 1978 by Joan and Richard Sweeney, titled "Monetary Theory and the Great Capitol Hill Baby-sitting Co-op Crisis." Krugman derives his monetary philosophy from this piece, but unfortunately he misunderstands the story entirely, and this leads him to draw erroneous conclusions about monetary and currency affairs.

The story is this: In the 1970s, a baby-sitting co-operative with

150 couples as members decided to issue coupons entitling the bearer to one hour of baby-sitting. After a while, it became apparent that "few coupons were in circulation—too few, in fact, to meet the co-op's needs." People were accumulating coupons, rather than "spending" them. Eventually, the governing board decided to issue more coupons, and—presto!—the co-op's "GBP—gross baby-sitting product, measured in units of babies sat—soared."

Krugman's conclusion is this: "Recessions . . . can be fought simply by printing money—and can sometimes (usually) be cured with surprising ease." Yet the lesson of the case is more complex, far more illuminating—and it contradicts Krugman's views on currency matters entirely.

A central authority—the co-op, in this case—decided to issue a currency that could be used only to barter time. First, this authority had to determine how many coupons should be issued to enable a liquid market. Let's assume here that seventy-five couples want to go out Friday nights and the other seventy-five Saturday nights, all at the same time. If only seventy-five coupons are issued, and nobody knows who owns them on a particular Friday or Saturday morning, many transactions will be waived because of the time needed to make the matches. The outcome is a baby-sitting depression, true. However, if 225 coupons are issued, half of the couples, on average, will be holding one coupon, the other half two coupons, and fewer transactions would be waived.

But notice that the printing of additional coupons—Krugman's suggested solution—solves this problem only because:

- the "central bank" made the initial mistake of issuing too few coupons;
- the "bank" had monopoly powers;
- there were no financial entrepreneurs within this group to create rights to coupons;
- people decided to forego the pleasure of going out rather than pay for baby-sitting services with cash (which would have had to come from their after-tax incomes).

If the experience of the baby-sitting group is correctly applied to monetary policy, the conclusions to be drawn, which are very different from Krugman's, are that:

- more constraints should be placed on central banks to prevent them from making big blunders to start with;
- the monopoly of central banks should re-examined;
- regulations in the financial sector may hinder problem solving;
- determining how much currency should be issued is hardly a trivial matter, since it depends on technology and regulations in financial markets (if the 150 families were on the Internet and had negotiated sophisticated financial contracts, the initial number of coupons would have become almost irrelevant).

These are exactly the conclusions reached in this chapter. Unfortunately, Krugman's utter misunderstanding of this case, which he has been using for years in his books and articles to illustrate his views on currency matters, is repeated in the rest of this book. Let's start with his analysis of the situation in Mexico in 1994. Krugman says that the Mexican authorities, faced with a steady drain of foreign-currency reserves, had to choose between raising interest rates or devaluing their currency. But as we saw, that's not quite what happened.

A massive printing of pesos preceded the steady outflow and the devaluation. Why did the Mexican central bank do that? And once the financial markets found this out, why didn't the bank sell bonds and absorb the unwanted peso liquidity? The answer is not that Mexico's central bankers did not know what they were doing, or that they considered (and rejected) the consequences of temporarily higher interest rates. In fact, the story was quite different.

The Mexican government was faced with a very inconvenient dilemma—and just before the national elections, too. Between June 1991 and July 1992, the government had sold eighteen banks. It provided full insurance coverage for almost all depositors, but it did not impose regulations on the quality of loans. Not surprisingly, bankers loaned with abandon to many of their friends. To keep the banks solvent, the government had to cover an unexpected US$70-billion bill when many of the loans—no surprise here—turned bad.

Mexican politicians had to either tell the just-about-to-go-to-vote public that they had made a big mistake, and that the taxpayers (rather than the banks' well-connected shareholders and bondholders) would have to foot the bill for it, or print the pesos and fulfill—nominally—the insurance-induced commitment. They opted for the latter. Then they tried to hide their decision for a while, so that a privileged few could take out their money—an estimated US$20 billion (the loss in foreign currency that Krugman mentions)—at still-favorable rates. Contrary to the conclusions reached by Krugman and many members of the press, the money was taken out not by "short-term foreign speculators," but by Mexican citizens. Once the abundance of unwanted pesos became noticeable, devaluation followed.

The government then called in the U.S. treasury–backed IMF, which used macroeconomic gobbledegook to sell the world on the idea of devaluation. The IMF's analysis of the situation made absolutely no reference to deposit insurance, inappropriate deregulation, political calculations, or even the technical alternative of selling bonds to absorb the unwanted pesos. Krugman says that Mexican policy-makers did not know what they were doing by "allowing the currency to become overvalued, expanding credit instead of tightening it when speculation against the peso began, and botching the devaluation itself in a way that unnerved investors." It is far more convenient politically to plead ignorance than it is to accept blame. Krugman never asks why the Mexican central bankers display such ignorance with a startling six-year regularity, which just happens to coincide with the national elections.

Now let's turn to Krugman's analysis of Japan. According to him, Japan is nothing but a "financial bubble [that] . . . burst." But does he provide the slightest evidence of this? None.

He makes no reference at all to the facts discussed earlier in this chapter: that between 1986 and 1990, the Bank of Japan pursued a lax monetary policy; and that, beginning in 1988, the government imposed a 20 percent withholding tax on savings, a capital gains tax on equity sales, a security transfer tax, a 3 percent consumption tax, a 6 percent tax on new cars, a 2.5 percent surtax on corporate profits, and that massive capital gains tax on real estate. The unexpected, rapid increases in taxes, combined with the sudden tightening of monetary policy, caused stock markets to fall.

Krugman makes no reference to any of this. Instead, he—like all those who think that governments and economists can match capital with talent more successfully than financial markets do—talks about irrational bubbles. Krugman says that Japan will be prosperous again if it simply pursues a 4 percent rate of inflation. For how long? He does not say. Will employees agree to a drop in real wages of more than 20 percent over five years? No mention. Even Krugman's occasional recommendation of 2 percent inflation means that money would lose half its value within thirty-five years—one generation. Why is that good?

It is toward the end of the book that Krugman's lack of understanding of basic monetary issues becomes even more troubling. He says that it is unclear why Australia was able to sail through the Asian crisis when Indonesia could not. His answer is that financial markets have a double standard. If they have confidence in a country, such as was the case with Australia, they will buy its currency after a plunge. But they sell currencies like Indonesia's when they plunge, exacerbating the lack of confidence.

Nonsense. Financial markets have always had one standard: trust. How quickly trust is restored once it is lost depends on the checks and balances in a country. No financial security can be created if there is not a good degree of trust.

Even corrupt governments have seen their currencies fall and recover quickly; Brazil is the most recent example of this. Yet the speed with which currencies recover has nothing to do with Krugman's rehashed Keynesian solutions; it has to do with the governments in question offering some signal that their monetary affairs would be placed in trusted hands. Brazil sent just such a signal when it named as its new central banker Armanio

Fraga, who for years was George Soros's trusted partner.

Let us finish by examining one final paragraph in the book, a paragraph that goes to the heart of Krugman's total misunderstanding of monetary affairs. He says that "right-wing critics of the IMF" are mistaken when they say that the organization "should have told countries to defend their original exchange rates at all costs." What does advocating the maintenance of the value of money have to do with ideology? Paper money is the government's non-interest-paying debt. It is a contract like all others. So why doesn't the principle of protecting property rights apply to this particular contract? Krugman advocates property rights in the abstract, but he seems to be unaware that the principle is linked to the maintenance of monetary standards.

Though a stable currency does not guarantee prosperity (mistaken fiscal and regulatory policies will cause capital to flow out even if a currency is stable, as we have seen so clearly in Argentina, its currency board notwithstanding), it is a necessary part of a vital capital market. But it takes discipline to maintain a country's currency as a monetary standard, and central banks cannot pursue both this goal and others. Perhaps the Bank of Canada's Web site reflects perfectly the confusion that exists today in monetary affairs. There, the bank describes its role, "as defined in the original Bank of Canada Act of 1934," as being "to promote the economic and financial well-being of Canada." Isn't that the role of governments?

Our central bankers want us to trust them to manage their countries' monetary affairs. But that trust is misplaced in a world where monetary policy has been politicized by either unaccountable and corrupt bureaucracies or those in the grip of political lies rationalized by faddish macroeconomic doctrines. The vague, all-encompassing "mission statement" quoted above reflects the latter trend.

It's time to get back to the fundamentals and refocus the central banks on maintaining the internal and external stability of their currencies, their true mission. Then we should return to fixed exchange rates (the Euro is, in a way, a step in that direction), re-establishing the monetary discipline and supporting institutions such a system demands. In fact, New Zealanders are now floating the idea of monetary union with Australia. And in Mexico, the debate about establishing a currency board or even adopting the U.S. dollar grows louder.

Mark Twain once said, "Customs are rock, laws are sand." The statement captures perfectly what happens in monetary matters when customary agreements among people are replaced by faddish dictates from the top. But sands can also be blown away easily. After more than a half-century of misguided monetary experiments, a return to fixed exchange rates will restore monetary "customs." Money will then once again be a trusted standard that will allow people to sign their contracts and carry out transactions by custom—unthinkingly, in other words.

CHAPTER 6

NATIONALISM

W*here do we get the absurd idea* that one of the best forms of social organization is one where political boundaries do not cross ethnic ones? In his book *Nationalism*, Elie Kedourie writes: "Nationalism . . . pretends to supply a criterion for the determination of the unit of population . . . to enjoy a government exclusively its own, for the legitimate exercise of power in the state, and for the right organization of a society of states. . . . [T]he doctrine holds that humanity is naturally divided into nations, that nations are known by certain characteristics which can be ascertained, and that the only legitimate type of government is national self-government."

How did this doctrine gain currency, first in Europe and then throughout the world, and produce the still internationally recognized principle of "self-determination"? Can the world be cured of this false doctrine? How do capital markets and international institutions enter into this picture? Can the U.S. play a role in correcting a mistake made by one of its own presidents, Woodrow Wilson, on this issue? Can we move from the principle of self-determination to one of equality before laws?

These questions are raised and answered in this chapter.

TRIBES AND NATIONS

Historians, philosophers, and social scientists identify nationalism as the dominant political force shaping the history of Europe over the past two centuries. "The triumph of nationalism is . . . the central reality of modern times," remarks the historian William McNeill. Norman Rich, in his *Age of Nationalism,* writes that this was the most pervasive ideological force in nineteenth-century Europe. "On the basis of the national principle," he suggests, "Germany and Italy were unified; the independence of Hungary was recognized; . . . Serbia, Montenegro, and Rumania were conceded complete independence from Turkish rule." But exactly what was new about nationalism in late-eighteenth- and nineteenth-century Europe?

People have always belonged to groups, distrusted strangers, resisted "contamination" by alien nations and races, and occasionally hated foreigners. There are two extreme ways of dealing with the disputes that result from such attitudes. One is to apply the principle of equality before laws, which requires the backing of many institutions before it can be put into practice—as we saw in earlier chapters. Once applied, however, this principle encourages trade and specialization, and brings about prosperity. The alternative is to pursue greater independence, erect barriers to interactions with other tribes, and guard against them.

But greater independence is costly. To maintain the independence of the tribe and still prosper, members must put forth a higher level of effort. And for this, they must be motivated by something more than personal gain. Fear can be a great motivator, and nationalism turned out to be a good method of sustaining fear in some circumstances (although occasionally it drove people overboard and into frenzies, which sometimes had dire consequences).

Consider for a moment what would happen if people trusted their neighbors more. They could then specialize to a greater extent, become richer, and thus rely more on both the self-interest and the occasional kindness of strangers. Increased specialization, when it's combined with open financial markets, brings about prosperity. But trust, like any other form of capital, is not free. Institutions must promote and sustain it. If such institutions do not exist or are destroyed, then trust, like all capital, will depreciate with time.

Lack of trust diminishes the size of markets, as well as people's incentive to specialize. To compensate for the loss and sustain their standards of living, while still isolating themselves from their neighbors, people must work harder and be motivated by something other than self-interest. Nationalism became this "something other."

In the Bible, the Jews were the "chosen people," the heirs of a proud civilization, who had to beware of the seductions of inferior cultures. Samson and Delilah's story is a metaphor for this: it's the tale of the fate of the wild, strong Hebrew man who is weakened when he succumbs to a harlot's charm—trusting when he should not, and literally letting his hair down. The exact same story is found in *The Epic of Gilgamesh,* the oldest surviving epic. It describes how Enkidu, the wild man of the steppes, is seduced by a harlot, a frequent symbol of inferior culture. Today's metaphors may differ from those of earlier centuries, but the lessons do not.

People are taught to trust members of their own tribe more than they do others. This makes them predisposed to sustaining occasional high levels of effort and making sacrifices for the group. Indeed, this is what the words "tribalism" and "nationalism" initially meant: powerful, voluntary connections and a readiness to sacrifice. The novelty of eighteenth- and nineteenth-century Europe was a doctrine that argued that people would be better off if political boundaries overlapped with tribal ones.

To validate this argument, writers and politicians of the nineteenth century reintroduced early musings on the subject. After all, linking nationalism, language, and race was not a nineteenth-century idea. The sixteenth-century Swiss historian Aegidius Tschudi differentiated the Swiss from the Germans by their race, and from the French by their language. He was not alone in his opinions. Historians had been making similar arguments all over Europe since the fourteenth century—probably without noticing how such arguments played into the hands of rulers who were interested in making their populations more insular and less mobile. With less mobility, people could be taxed more. And can anything make people more immobile than a distinct language? The fewer the lines of communication, the less likely it is that people will co-operate and become a threat to the status quo. Of course, the establishment will disguise its true motives when creating barriers to communication—that's what the lessons of the story of the Tower of Babel were meant to be. That story taught us that common language can foster co-operation and great ambition. But at what price? This is the same story that the nationalists of the nineteenth and twentieth centuries wanted to teach, playing (inadvertently, perhaps) right into the hands of rulers, who have always been eager to immobilize their subjects by any means possible.

Nation-states were not an eighteenth- and nineteenth-century invention either. The nation-states of antiquity included Egypt, Persia, Rome, Macedon, and ancient Israel. However, all of these became empires within very short periods of time, and they all ruled over a diversity of people. This was the normal situation. The Romans, for example, knew that they could hold on to power only if they brought conquered populations to their side, encouraged intermarriages between Roman soldiers and "locals," and were suspicious of tribes (i.e., the Hebrews) who discouraged such intermarriages.

Until the fifteenth century, there were also the European nation-states of Denmark, Sweden, Poland, Hungary, and France. Again, the idea that there were advantages to be had in ruling over just one ethnic group did not exist here. Poland, for example, wanted to attract traders. In fact, a large number of Germans (German Jews, in particular) were given special privileges in return for settling there.

We can see, then, that the existence of social organizations called "nation-states" was nothing new. Instead, what led to the sudden rise of nationalism—that is, a movement in favor of overlapping political boundaries with ethnic ones—was the rapid increase in Europe's population and the mistrust this demographic change brought out among Europe's "tribes."

EUROPEAN EVENTS OF THE EIGHTEENTH AND NINETEENTH CENTURIES: DEMOGRAPHY IS NOT DESTINY, BUT . . .

France became Europe's most populous country during the eighteenth century. But during the nineteenth century, its growth slowed and its population grew older. Most of its neighbors, meanwhile, especially the various members of the Hapsburg Empire, saw fertility levels and population figures rise.

Some numbers briefly summarize—albeit somewhat superficially—the significant changes in the demographic picture of Europe of the eighteenth and nineteenth centuries. France's population in 1700 was 21 million; in 1800 it was 29 million, and by 1900 it had grown to 41 million. Prussia's population jumped from 1.75 million in 1700 to nine million in 1800. During the nineteenth century, it dominated all other German states. In 1834, it formed a customs union, and then, in 1871, it became an empire. The German confederation, meanwhile, had a population of 35 million in 1850 and 57 million in 1900. For most other European nations, population at least doubled during the nineteenth century. A period of rapid population growth among one's not fully trusted neighbors has always sparked fear, especially during times when wealth was derived from the land.

Significant political changes began to sweep through Europe with the French Revolution in 1789. The revolution began to define a citizen as French not by his language, religion, or ethnicity, but by his commitment to the new political institutions. Language, which was to be singled out during the nineteenth century as the basis for nationhood and the foundation of nationalism,

135

was not a criterion for belonging to the newly defined French nation. In 1789, 50 percent of Frenchmen did not speak French at all (in the north and south, nobody spoke it), and only 12 percent of the rest spoke it "correctly."

But the French of the revolutionary era did not need a uniform language to see that they had things in common. Indeed, a sense of nationality had been percolating among those living under the French kings' rule since the fifteenth century. This happened because of both the Hundred Years War, which united the French against their common enemy (England), and the continuous growth of France's central government, which supplanted local institutions. Also, with the exception of a small number of Jews, France was a Catholic country. (The mistrusted, entrepreneurial Huguenots had been expelled by the end of the seventeenth century.)

The revolution only strengthened these ties. For the French citizens of the newly defined "nation," the slogan Liberty, Equality, Fraternity came to represent the freedom to oppose the status quo, and to expect compensation and solutions through institutional change. Simon Schama, in his 1989 book *Citizens,* remarks that when people "were told that a true national assembly would . . . provide satisfaction, they were given a direct stake in sweeping institutional change. This was exactly what happened in late 1788 and early 1789." The new French "nation" was held together not only by the past—that is, language and ethnicity—but also by the future.

In addition to transforming institutions and laws, the revolutionary government introduced the conscription ballot, which resulted in a vastly expanded army and thus increased state power. In March 1793, the Committee of Public Safety decreed the *levée en masse,* and was assigned three-hundred thousand men. The decree was accompanied by further centralization, and in this way the government usurped powers from local administrations.

What did the transformation of France mean to the rest of Europe? Here was a country that had lost almost every war during the eighteenth century, was humiliated during the Seven Years War, and by 1789 was too poor to maintain its maritime and continental military forces. But just three years later, in 1792, it declared war on Austria and Prussia. By November of the same year, its armies had invaded the Austrian Netherlands (today's Belgium), Savoy, and some of the principalities of the Rhineland. The occupying armies secured the loyalty of many in the occupied lands by establishing regimes based on the principles of the French Revolution, especially the abolition of class privileges and the weakening of traditional "tribal" ties. Though the European powers formed repeated coalitions against France, they were defeated. Between 1806 and 1812, most European nations were a part of the French Empire, were under French control, or had become French allies.

The totally unexpected, spectacular military successes of Europe's most populous state—a state that was bankrupt just twelve years before—led statesmen and the elite of Europe to look closely at its institutional changes and military strategies. They wanted to see what had provoked such heights of national enterprise and how such an effort could be sustained. They reached the conclusion that mass conscript armies, centralization, and the myth of national destiny were the means by which increased numbers of people could be united. Or rather, re-united.

Nationalism seemed an ideology capable of uniting people whose traditional ties had been weakened, and who were surrounded by increasing numbers of "other" people (whom they distrusted greatly). Rulers expected that the strengthened domestic ties would help their nations resist military threats and misgovernment by foreigners. There is nothing new in this phenomenon. At one time, religion played a similar role. Remember that the word "religion" comes from *religare,* which means to "re-link."

RE-LINKING PEOPLE
When nationalism first rose as an ideology, German- and Italian-speaking people were widely scattered over Central, Eastern, and Southern Europe in free cities, ecclesiastical states, and small principalities. Polish-speaking people lived in three empires (Russia,

Austria-Hungary, and Prussia), and Italians lived in a variety of provinces and small states (some under Austrian rule). Not surprisingly, German, Italian, and Polish philosophers and writers espoused the notion that "language was the only adequate indicator of nationality," and that political frontiers that separated people speaking a common language were "unnatural," "arbitrary," and "unjust."

Although, politically speaking, there was no German nation in 1807, the influential Johann Gottlieb Fichte wrote, in his *Addresses to the German Nation,* that "the separation of Prussians from the rest of the Germans is purely artificial." The Italian Giuseppe Mazzini, a pioneer of the doctrine of nationalism, wrote, while in exile in Marseilles, that "there is no international question as to the forms of government, but only a national question."

Such theories had influence because some Europeans had to bear the twin burdens of taxes and the continuous military threats of Napoleon. For other Europeans, those in the Austro-Hungarian Empire, the same theories became a tool with which mistrusted Vienna's oppression could be fought.

However, neither the burdens nor the oppression would have been a sufficient conduit for the spread of the nationalist doctrine. Such burdens were nothing new, and philosophers had offered nationalist theories before the nineteenth century. But the nineteenth century marked the first time that misgovernment *came together* with the lessons of the French Revolution. The revolution showed that it was possible to unite a great number of people around a new idea (nationalism) and provoke enthusiasm, which would in turn encourage these people to stand firm against mistrusted foreigners and lead to the reshaping of domestic institutions.

In other words, since neither the French nor the Hapsburgs moved to build up trust among the many European tribes (though some expected Napoleon to do this, and thus initially welcomed the French invasion), greater independence was the obvious alternative.

The unification of Germany—along with its surprising military successes against Denmark, Austria, even France, and its economic successes too—lent further credence to the idea that the promotion of a national consciousness based on both language and a common past (real and imagined) was the key to a group's success. Here is how Paul Kennedy, in his book *The Rise and Fall of the Great Powers*, summarized the commonly held views of the characteristic features of the rising powers of Europe, as well as those of powers that declined during the nineteenth century:

> At least 90 percent of Frenchmen spoke French and the same proportion belonged at least nominally to the Catholic Church. More than eight in every ten Prussians were German (the rest were mostly Poles), and of the Germans 70 percent were Protestant. The Tsar's seventy million subjects included some notable minorities (five million Poles, three and a half million Finns, Ests, Letts and Latvians, and three million assorted Caucasians), but that still left fifty million who were both Russian and Orthodox. And the inhabitants of the British Isles were 90 percent English-speaking and 70 percent Protestant. Countries like this needed little holding together; they had an intrinsic cohesion. By contrast the Austrian Emperor ruled an ethnic mishmash. . . . He and eight million of his subjects were German, but twice as many were Slavs of one sort or another (Czechs, Slovaks, Poles, Ruthenians, Slovenes, Croats, Serbs), five million were Hungarians, five million Italians and two million Romanians. What sort of nation did that make? The answer is none at all.

Moreover, the declining Ottoman Empire stood as evidence that somehow provoked "homogeneity" works, but multi-ethnicity does not.

These statistics are an oversimplification, however, since Germany was a federal state where the constitutional debates of the nineteenth century focused on the dangers of centralization and the necessity of maintaining the "special characteristics of the tribes."

But federalist principles did not counterbalance the view that nationalism is the best foundation for social organizations, since the shared view was that federations had weak governments and could not withstand military threats.

De Tocqueville, in his *Democracy in America,* shared this view, and wrote that although federalism was "the most powerful combination favoring human prosperity and freedom," it was inappropriate for Europe, since Europeans had wars to fear, which the Americans did not. De Tocqueville refused to believe that, in a battle with equal force on either side, a confederated nation could withstand a nation with centralized government power. He observed, "A nation that divided its sovereignty when faced by the great military monarchies of Europe would seem to me, by that single act, to be abdicating its power, and perhaps its existence and its name."

Indeed, the American military in 1860 consisted of 26,000 personnel; in 1880, it was 36,000. In Europe during those same twenty years, the numbers ranged between 347,000 and 248,000 in the U.K., 608,000 and 544,000 in France, 862,000 and 909,000 in Russia, 201,000 and 430,000 in Germany, and 306,000 and 273,000 in the Hapsburg Empire. It is no accident that the army became the essential institution of Otto von Bismarck's Germany. Militarized nationalism was the heart and soul of German unification.

These events during the eighteenth and nineteenth centuries helped establish nationalism as a credible political doctrine in Germany and Italy, re-linking their populations in a Europe whose many increasingly populous tribes mistrusted one another. At the same time, the oppression of minorities within the Austro-Hungarian Empire fuelled national aspirations among the smaller groups found within its borders. In other words, a growing mistrust *among* tribes provoked a tightening of links *within* increasingly populous tribes.

One problem with the nationalist doctrine has been that even when political independence was achieved and misgovernment by strangers disappeared, centralization on the basis of nationalist principles stayed, and thus the demand for rationales to maintain and expand policies based on these principles remained. Ideas have long lives, and they often outlive their usefulness when they're embodied in institutions. Nineteenth-century Europe saw the establishment of the great national museums, theaters, and public schools, all of which presented or taught imaginary "national" histories that had suspicion of strangers at their core. As a result, centralization created a wide variety of groups—in addition to the army and its related industries—that became interested in sustaining "nationalist" theories, and had no interest in moving to establish institutions to restore trust among "strangers." Like other theoreticians of nationalism, Friedrich List, an economist and a German "national" hero, supplied the rationales for centralization, rationales that those in power promoted as scientific theories with eternal, universal validity.

Thus ideas that were initially useful in fighting misgovernment by foreigners, and that were a response to the growing mistrust within each increasingly populous tribe, were transformed into harmful myths that led to centralization and (ironically) more misgovernment.

Later, these same ideas became obstacles to restoring trust and opening up capital markets. Social scientists, philosophers, intellectuals, and members of the cultural elite became part of the myth-making industry, and worked to sustain centralization based on nationalist doctrines. The policies of the great European powers, meanwhile, added fuel to the fire, encouraging myths about the advantages of nationalism as a general political doctrine.

NATIONALISM AMONG SMALLER NATIONS

I do not know how the conflicting territorial claims of Romanians, Greeks, Serbs, Albanians, Turks, and others would have been settled if they had been left on their own at the end of the nineteenth century and the beginning of the twentieth. But they were not left alone.

Russia declared war on Turkey, on behalf of the Bulgars (thus shaping Bulgaria's borders), in 1877; later, Germany helped Turkish ambitions (thus shaping Turkish borders). In 1908, Austria annexed Bosnia and Herzegovina, which Serbia wanted and thought to get with Russian support. But the Russians could not help because they had been humiliated in a 1904–5 war by Japan, yet another homogeneous, populous, demographically young nation-state. In his book *The History of Western Civilization,* William McNeill summarizes briefly several additional conflicts, identifying their consequences for both the smaller nations and the great powers. He writes:

> In 1912 another Balkan crisis arose as a consequence of the successful war which the Christian states of that peninsula (Serbia, Montenegro, Bulgaria and Greece) fought against the Turks. . . . This crisis, too, was surmounted without general European war. Even when the victors quarreled over the spoils and a second Balkan war broke out (1913) that pitted Serbia, Greece, Rumania and Turkey against Bulgaria, prompt capitulation on the part of Bulgaria forestalled any widening of the disturbance. Each time one or the other of the great powers backed down in a crisis, its leaders resolved . . . also to prepare militarily so that a further diplomatic setback need not be endured. Consequently a growing arms race developed among the major powers. When the Germans began to build a navy, the British decided to outbuild them; when a new and more efficient type of warship—the dreadnought—was introduced, both Germans and British decided to build more of them than the other did. . . . The size of standing armies was increased by prolonging the period of training to which conscripts were subjected; and the decisions of one government came to be tied to the decisions made by a rival.

By this time, the disadvantages of sustaining nationalist myths had become evident. Yet in spite of this failure, which culminated in the

First World War, the principle of self-determination and the legitimacy of nation-states seemed to triumph. Let us see why.

PRINCIPLES AND, ONCE AGAIN, DEMOGRAPHY

A glimpse at the demographic map of modern-day Europe and other parts of the world shows that ambitions based on nationalist principles are often in conflict because people move and do not live in isolated, compact territories. In what was once Yugoslavia, for example, about 9 million Serbs, 4.7 million Croats, and 10 million others (Albanians, Hungarians, Slovenes, Macedonians, Montenegrins, and Bosnian Muslims) intermingle. What was for seventy-four years Czechoslovakia has also been transformed. Today, there are 10.5 million living in the Czech Republic and five million living in Slovakia (of which 600,000 are Hungarians). This demographic distribution is already the result of the 1945 expulsion of 2.4 million Sudeten Germans, who did not flee when the Russians came in. Meanwhile, in the midst of Azerbaijan (whose majority is Muslim), there is the Nagorno-Karabakh enclave with its 150,000 Armenians (who are Christians). In the south of Armenia, at the Iranian border, there is Nakhichevan, which belongs to Azerbaijan, though there is no territorial continuity. The former Soviet Union's five central Asian republics (Kazakstan, Kyrgyzstan, Tajikistan, Turkmenistan, and Uzbekistan) all have mixed, intermingled populations.

Such demographic patterns are neither unusual nor particular to empires. Switzerland's population is 65 percent German-, 18 percent French-, 10 percent Italian-, and one percent Rhaeto-Romance-speaking. Yet these diverse people share a pleasant existence, and shared it even when France and Germany were at each other's throats. In 1910, by contrast, the fifty-two million inhabitants of what was the Austro-Hungarian Empire did not share a pleasant existence. They were 23.9 percent Germans, 20 percent Magyars, 12 percent Czechs, 10 percent Poles, 4 percent Slovaks, 5 percent Croats, 3.8 percent Serbs, 7.9 percent Ruthenians, 6.4 percent Romanians, 2.6 percent Slovenes, 2 percent Italians, and 1.2 percent Muslim Serbo-Croats.

What do such patterns tell us about the principle of self-determination? Does it lead to decentralization and regionalism? Does self-determination imply that any group has the right to secede, taking territory with it? Does it imply only the right of migration? Or does it imply the right to exchange populations as if they were property (as happened between Greece and Turkey)? Conceivably—given the number of languages spoken in the approximately two hundred states that currently exist—we could be faced with a world of eight thousand nation-states.

President Woodrow Wilson's administration did not raise these questions when it committed itself to the idea of self-determination after the First World War. Nor were they addressed years later when the idea found its way into the United Nations' 1970 Declaration on Principles of International Law, which made a predictably unsatisfactory distinction between the right of self-determination and the right of secession.

Whatever President Wilson's personal views, his administration's interest in self-determination was pragmatic. The Americans hoped that the new nation-states emerging from the collapse of the Austro-Hungarian Empire would counterbalance the German nation-state. At the same time, they hoped that nationalism would prove to be a strong competitor to the Communist doctrine. After all, Communism and nationalism shared the same goals: to link people, demand their loyalty, and obtain political legitimacy. But unlike nationalism, Communism was based on the notion that there is an insurmountable animosity between classes (rather than tribes), and that allegiance to social class would dominate allegiances to ethnicity, religion, language, and culture. The option of moving toward institutions that would encourage trade and inspire greater trust among the rich and the poor—by allowing the poor to become rich and the rich to fall from their pedestals (something that democratized financial markets achieve)—was never considered.

Unfortunately, the members of Wilson's administration had miscalculated. The policy prevented neither German nor Communist aggression. Adherence to the abstract principle of self-determination also showed that establishing small nations did not necessarily solve the problems of even smaller ones, which now found themselves within new borders. They were called minorities, which adroitly deflected their claim to nationhood and self-determination. Language is indeed an effective weapon.

The internationally recognized principle might even have made things worse by raising the expectations of any group that had grievances. In the name of self-determination, these groups could now appeal for restitution, change, and redress to the new great powers (which, when it was in their interests, were happy to comply). But such expectations could only start conflicts or prevent them from being settled more quickly. The events leading to the First World War are an example of how this happened in the past. Recent events in what was Yugoslavia are a modern day reminder. To quote Mark Twain again: history rhymes.

REPEATING MISTAKES

Fights were already under way in 1992 when the European Community, as part of a German initiative, decided to recognize the separate republics of Croatia and Slovenia. But the German initiative was driven by factors other than a simple desire to recognize one's neighbors, including Helmut Kohl's cajoling for votes at home. The majority of Yugoslavs who work in Germany come from Croatia, as is the case with most Germans of Yugoslav origin (who came there as migrants in the inter-war period). And since both Croatia and Slovenia had traditional ties with Germany (the Croats were some of Germany's most obliging and savage collaborators during the Second World War), the new countries seemed to be not only potential allies, but also friendly places to export and invest.

The means by which the German government persuaded its European Community partners to support its initiative are by now of no practical interest (though it is useful to note that France, the Netherlands, and the U.K. were initially against such recognition). It is now also too late to say that Washington's recognition of Croatia and Slovenia was another miscalculation. Indeed,

Washington had originally opposed the recognition, but it later reversed itself, probably to keep a common front with the European Community in the name of the "New World Order."

It is difficult to accept the argument that the U.S. reversed itself because it believed Serbia's Slobodan Milosevic was an aggressive nationalist with Communist tendencies, whereas Croatia's Franjo Tudjman was an innocent democrat on the defensive. Tudjman was no white lily. He passed Croatia's citizenship laws, which practically prohibited non-Croats from attaining citizenship no matter how long they lived there. Mistrust in that corner of the world has been reigning for centuries.

Subsequent events in Croatia and Serbia show how domestic politics among the great powers prolong conflicts instead of resolving them, especially when those politics intermingle with the principle of self-determination. The West's move to recognize Croatia's independence probably led the Croat leaders to expect two things: that the recognition implied not just words but deeds too, and that it would weaken the negotiating power of the Serbs. They miscalculated too.

The situation in Yugoslavia illustrates in an additional way how politics prolong ethnic conflicts. Before Communism fell and ethnic strife began in Yugoslavia, the West embraced what appeared to be the most liberal of the Communist lands—albeit in the hope of destabilizing the Communist bloc. The aid sent by the West to the central government in Belgrade was sufficient to keep a lid on the deep-running ethnic antagonisms—and subsidize, in fact, Marshal Tito and his fellow Communists. The aid and preferential treatment vanished, however, once Yugoslavia ceased to be of use in the global power play. And what happened? The ethnic conflicts, which had once been drowned with money, resurfaced—as has happened repeatedly in that part of the world.

NATIONALISM AND CENTRALIZATION

By the end of the nineteenth century, there were politicians in the Hapsburg Empire who saw that nationalism was, at least in part, a reaction to centralization. At that time, as Paul Kennedy put it, "Vienna's classic answer to all . . . particularist grievances was to smother them with commitments, with new jobs, tax concessions, additional railway branch lines, and so on. There were, in 1914, well over three million civil servants, running things as diverse as schools, hospitals, welfare, taxation, railways, post, etc." These were bribes, and to Canada and other modern "nation-building" states the consequences should stand as a warning. When central governments seek to maintain attachments by bribing people with favors, the result is centralization, discontent, distrust, and the rise of nationalist sentiment. On the other hand, when power is re-allocated from the center to strengthen diversity, it re-establishes trust and brings prosperity (under the conditions discussed below).

The Austrian Karl Renner, who was foreign minister after the First World War and also the first president of the reborn Austrian Republic (from 1945 to 1950), devised a solution to rising nationalism. He advocated the transformation of the Hapsburg Empire into a federal, democratic state. He also thought it necessary to confine nationalism to the spheres of culture and communications, thus separating it from territorial questions just as the Church had been separated from the State. To achieve this goal, he argued that the economic sphere should cross national boundaries, and that there should be a central, supranational government. In a way, Renner was anticipating features of the European Community. He also suggested redrawing the empire's maps around counties that were homogeneous in language, which according to him would have solved the nationalist problem in nine-tenths of the empire.

In places where people were too intermingled to be separated, Renner suggested special provisions to guarantee equal rights and an impartial administration. His precise idea was that each individual, no matter where he lived, should be a member of an ethnic organization that had agencies all over the empire (much like the Catholic Church, once it became independent of the State). Renner was not successful in carrying out his ideas, however. The consequences of Woodrow Wilson's policies and principles were just some of the many obstacles he faced.

147

We cannot know now whether Renner's plan would have provided a permanent solution for ethnic rivalries. But it seemed plausible, especially since it focused on decentralizing and depoliticizing cultural issues (i.e., giving a far smaller role to government and a larger one to voluntary organizations). Are there any political-institutional arrangements that were tried and actually succeeded in diminishing ethnic, religious, and linguistic conflicts?

SOLUTIONS

One system that has been pursued with obvious success is the melting pot of the federal U.S. government—an example of a state creating, in the course of time, a new, larger tribe with the most open financial markets in the world. When American financial markets were closed to some groups, such as African Americans, symptoms of the aggressive "tribalism" that was common in eighteenth- and nineteenth-century Europe surfaced there too. Militant organizations, whose goal was to rebuild the strength of these marginalized groups, soon emerged.

But at the same time, events such as the civil rights movement were also helping to restore trust between the many "tribes" living under the U.S.'s federal umbrella. These new institutions were successful in transforming governments into a source of capital for these groups when private capital markets stayed closed. The debate today in the U.S. asks whether capital markets have now been opened sufficiently to members of these groups, and thus whether governments should no longer single them out for preferential treatment. In broad terms, then, the history of racial unrest in the U.S. over the past few decades can also be seen from the viewpoints advanced in this chapter and in chapter one. By looking at societies from the perspective of the "five sources of capital," one can predict the maze of complex conflicts that entangle societies when capital markets are closed and mistrust rises.

Countries such as Canada, Spain, Belgium, and Switzerland have pursued other types of solutions. Though they have each faced conflicts of their own, their problems pale in comparison with those of other multi-ethnic states, such as Russia, the Balkans, and several African and Asian nations. It is no accident that the Western states have, on the whole, found the more stable solutions. They had both open capital markets and more checks on government power. But when these key principles were forgotten, even the Western countries found themselves in trouble. Canada's Pierre Trudeau, for example, thought that imposed bilingualism was the key to diffusing rising Quebec nationalism and dispersing French Quebecers all over Canada. He combined this policy with high taxes, increased federal spending, and a general move toward a far more centralized model of government. Canada is still paying the price for this utterly misguided effort. French Quebecers did not move to other provinces. The English community of Quebec moved out, making the province even more "French" than it was before. And Canada still lives with high levels of taxing and spending, and has fallen significantly behind the U.S. in its standard of living.

Other parts of the world failed to learn the lessons. Today, countless governments spend money and resources on "nation building"—in, of all places, multilingual, multi-ethnic, and multi-tribal Third World countries. This is no real surprise, of course, given that Africa's population has exploded, and that many nations there lack the background needed to move toward trust-restoring institutions. As happened in Europe in previous centuries, the growing distrust we see in Africa today gives rise to the view that only independence can assure survival. Thus Cameroon is desperately trying to build national unity by transferring money between tribes. Its two hundred tribes speak 124 languages and dialects and share four religions. People communicate among themselves in English or French, and they live within arbitrary borders drawn in the sand by France, England, Germany, and Belgium—borders that nevertheless are accepted as sacred. Forcing or bribing people into building nations did not, does not, and will not work.

So what can be done?

In addition to inducing these countries to open up their financial markets (as a precondition for either aid or forgiving debts), we should pursue Karl Renner's suggestions. To diminish inter-group tensions, he recommended that nationalism be confined to the spheres of culture and communications. He saw people joining voluntary organizations that would then be responsible for linguistic, cultural, and educational matters. He believes that rights should be granted to individuals, but not to either groups or cultures. If people want religious education, education in an ethnic language, television programs and theater productions, or any other cultural institution, let them pay for it, voluntarily, from their after-tax incomes. Government involvement results in significantly increased spending at best, costly conflicts at worst. Though such an arrangement seems utopian today, when governments routinely decide on such issues with often only symbolic public input, we should recall that the inseparability of Church and State was once taken for granted as well.

The aforementioned arrangement would result in decentralization, which would in turn replace the principles of both self-determination and minority rights. Perhaps Václav Havel best summarizes the key features of such a society:

> No member of a single race, a single nation, a single sex, or a single religion may be endowed with basic rights that are any different from anyone else's. In other words, I am in favor of what is called a civic society. Today this civic principle is sometimes presented as if it stood in opposition to the principle of national affiliation, creating the impression that it ignores or suppresses the aspect of our home represented by our nationality. This is crude misunderstanding of that principle. On the contrary I support the civic principle because it represents the best way for individuals to realize themselves. . . . To establish a state on any other principle than the civic principle—on the principle of nationality, or religion, for instance—means making one aspect of our home superior to all the others, and thus reduces us as people, reduces our natural world. . . . Most wars and revolutions

. . . came about precisely because of this one-dimensional conception of the state.

Countries and regions that adhere to the one-dimensional notion of the state will fall behind those that adhere to the civic principle. If chapter one reached the conclusion that the U.S. will continue to thrive because of its open capital markets, this chapter only reinforces that conclusion, for the U.S. has also been moving in the right direction where its internal "tribal" conflicts are concerned. If it had adhered in its foreign policy to this principle as well, in addition to promoting democratized capital markets, the Balkan tragedy and many others might have been mitigated. As the sole remaining superpower, the U.S. is in a position today to force countries to which it provides aid or gives trading benefits to open their capital markets and quash demands for minority rights and self-determination.

We all have overlapping loyalties to family, friends, and ethnic and religious groups, and when these groups make conflicting demands on us, we solve them in our own particular way. The grave problems start when governments force us to give priority to one particular loyalty based on genes, the accident of birth, or the language we grew up with, and when they force us to sustain mythologies to rationalize such prioritization.

CHAPTER 7

EXTRACTING SUNBEAMS OUT OF CUCUMBERS

The title of this chapter comes from Jonathan Swift's *Gulliver's Travels*. When Gulliver arrives in the country of Laputa, the place is in ruin. But the academics are working on how to extract sunbeams out of cucumbers. Not much new under the sun.

How do ideas that have no foundation gain scientific status and get financed by governments? How can social scientists apparently believe sincerely that what they do is scientific when it is not? How do such theories gain influence and shape the terms of public debate? These are the questions that arise when we consider the facts and events presented in the previous chapters. The next two chapters give answers to these questions. But first, let us just make it clear what it means to pass along ideas that have no scientific status.

The June 9, 2000, issue of the *Wall Street Journal,* in an article on the Microsoft antitrust case, contains the following startling statement: "The Clinton administration's top economist, Treasury Secretary Lawrence Summers . . . gave an intriguing speech in San Francisco last month, titled 'The New Wealth of Nations,' that suggested that the proliferation of natural monopolies is more good than bad. In an information-based economy, he said, 'the only incentive to produce anything is the possession of temporary monopoly power—because without that power the price will be bid down to the marginal cost and the high initial fixed costs cannot be recouped. . . . So the constant pursuit of that monopoly power becomes the central driving thrust of the New Economy.' "

The strange thing in this paragraph is that Summers considers this pursuit "new," and that the *Wall Street Journal*'s correspondent considers Summers's statements "intriguing." Where have they been living? Five minutes spent in the company of any serious investor or venture capitalist—and not just today, but also decades and probably centuries ago—would have revealed that neither would put up a penny for any venture unless the entrepreneur behind it could convince him of the "enduring uniqueness" of his planned business. Why does this come as a surprise for someone with a Ph.D. in economics?

Every business venture incurs some fixed costs (R&D expenses, in particular), and most entrepreneurs cannot avoid making mistakes. Unless there is a promise of some lasting uniqueness—a temporary monopoly—all ventures will be considered losing propositions, and nobody will finance them. So what's intriguing here? And where is the novelty exactly?

Ironically, the novelty isn't in the world of business at all, but is in the strange arena of what passes for academic research in the economic profession. As recently as April 1998, John Kenneth Galbraith, a long-term resident of Harvard's economics department (with which Summers was also associated in his academic days), confessed in an interview that he had removed some of his books from course reading lists because he no longer believed the arguments. But he still considered the collapse of Communism to be one of the biggest disappointments of his life. What are economists teaching that can lead to statements like Galbraith's and Summers's?

Let's take a look at the regularly published *Microeconomics Reading Lists,* which presents the reading lists of the microeconomics courses offered at seventy-two major colleges and universities (including UCLA, Harvard, MIT, Northwestern, Minnesota, Columbia, Chicago, Pennsylvania, and Miami). It shows that in most of these places, what is being taught is "exactitude"—that is, models detached from all experience, and especially from reference to financial principles. In this detached world, Summers's statement *is* new. And since accountability and checks and balances do not figure in Galbraith's lexicon, his statements are not very surprising, either.

What does "teaching exactitude" mean? It means presenting the logic of models. But if a person wants to teach science—social science, in particular—she had better present not just models, but also evidence of how those models match up with the real world. Teaching social science without relating it to real-world events is a poor but all too common approach.

The content of the microeconomics courses mentioned above—an example of this poor approach in practice—makes sense of the comments of the *Wall Street Journal* reporter. For example, several of these courses focus on justifying government intervention on various grounds, through theories of "market failure," of "externalities," of "pure public goods." The reading lists include the theories of Paul Samuelson and Francis Bator, and many more recent economists. Not one reading list includes articles that discuss legal obstacles to financial markets that result in governments venturing into the void. Also, not one reading list includes Nobel Prize–winner Ronald Coase's "The Lighthouse in Economics," which is one of the few articles in this field that confronts the theories with facts.

In his article, Coase wrote that he chose the example of the lighthouse because economists often use it to explain the need for government to be a financial intermediary. Economists have argued that no private individual or firm would ever build and maintain a lighthouse, since the private sector could never secure payment from the owners of ships, and thus the venture would always be unprofitable. But Coase examined the history of the British Lighthouse System, and he showed that there was no correspondence between the actual situation and what economists from Mill, Sidgwick, and Pigou to Samuelson had long speculated about in models that were supposed to be based on features of the lighthouse industry. Private-sector lighthouses had existed for centuries.

Coase thus raises this question: "How is it that these great men have, in their economic writings, been led to make statements about lighthouses which are misleading as to the facts, whose meaning, if thought about in a concrete fashion, is quite unclear, and which, to the extent that they imply a policy conclusion, are very likely wrong? The explanation is that these references by economists to lighthouses are not the result of their having made a study of lighthouses or having read a detailed study by some other economist. . . . The lighthouse is simply plucked out of the air."

Coase's article was first published in 1974, but the erroneous discussion of the lighthouse is still in the textbooks decades later. Economics students are well acquainted with this example and its policy implications, and they arrive at the intended but utterly misleading conclusion. The frequently repeated idea thus passes for fact, and becomes part of a myth.

These microeconomics courses also cover "general equilibrium" models, all of which are based on the assumption that people are "risk-averse," and none of which makes reference to finance, innovation, and the commercialization of ideas. New ideas, in technology, management, the arts, or the sciences, do not make an appearance in these models because in a world of "general equilibrium," everything has already been invented—whatever that means. Why anyone should want to examine the trivial mathematics of a world of such thoughtless paradise, I do not know. And in this use of the term, "risk-averse" refers not to people who do not like to lose money (and are thus averse to "downside risk," to use the vocabulary of business magazines), but to people who never gamble, never buy a lottery ticket, and only insure themselves. None of these "general equilibrium" models holds true if there are members of society who have a "preference for risk," and who, as a result, gamble. But the gambling sector is booming all over the world. And that raises the same question Coase raised: How is it that so many economists (Kenneth Arrow and Gerard Debreu, two Nobel Prize winners, among them) have developed esoteric theories about human behavior that are misleading, inaccurate, and thus likely to inspire erroneous policies?

The answer is the same as the one Coase gave. Not one of these economists or any of their numerous followers has ever conducted even one study of actual gambling behavior. The general equilibrium theory was plucked from some economists' writings, but it did not include any factual examinations.

This general pattern characterizes the entire content of this central course in economics. The result is not only that "truth" is not being taught, but that a lie—call it by the better-sounding word "myth," if you like—*is* being taught, exactly, logically, and with great rigor and solemnity. Students are not being taught science; instead, they are being taught obscure linguistic exercises masquerading as science. Extracting sunbeams out of cucumbers, indeed.

It's an abuse of the language to use the words "models" and "theories" to describe what has been taught. At best, this should have been called logical speculation. These words would have drawn attention to the essence of what was being taught: people's unconfirmed, logical ideas and nothing more. This might have allowed students to doubt, be skeptical, test their teachers' views. But the words "model" and "theory" have suggested to naive and mediocre students that such ideas shed light on the world around them when they actually do not. Still, if all this had no implications outside the academic world, this whole matter would be of little interest. But words and ideas have consequences, as we have seen in the previous chapters.

HOW DO NON-SCIENTIFIC IDEAS GAIN SCIENTIFIC CREDIBILITY?

Matching ideas to real-world events is the meaning of being "scientific." It is unscientific to either ignore or reject—for no logical or empirical reason—discovered patterns of behavior. The results are bad science and pasts falsely imagined.

How have unscientific ideas gained currency? Does this happen in the social sciences only or also in other fields of inquiry? The answer, of course, is that it happens in all fields of human inquiry, and science is no exception. But as far as the sciences are concerned, some broad regularities can be detected. First, an academic comes up with an erroneous, obscure idea. If it's convenient, the establishment embraces it and subsidizes it. This has the effect of making the idea more and more complex, shrouding it in a heavy curtain of language. Some then mistake the obscure, pompous language for science.

By the time a few brave individuals announce that the king is naked, a large bureaucracy has been established. Its proponents use the blindly accepted unclear language to ridicule the innovators. The resulting obscurity doesn't harm its authors—who are now called social scientists—but protects them from public scrutiny. Aesop was right: "Obscurity often brings safety." Chapter four showed us how.

Persistence in Error

When Copernicus came up with his startling new story of the heavens, the critics asked, "Who will place the authority of Copernicus above that of the Holy Scripture?" It is not surprising, considering the power of religious institutions in those days, that Copernicus circulated part of his writings among his friends only, and did not even want to publish them during his lifetime. The result was that the Holy Scripture's view of the heavens continued to play center stage, and Copernicus's view stayed out of sight.

Galileo did publish a defense of Copernican theory, and was sentenced to life imprisonment. What was happening at that time in "science"? The prestige of the science was rising, while that of the Jesuits—who had their own "scientific theories"—was declining (though they still had much political and financial clout). Still, the Jesuits were ready to fight not only new ideas (if they were inconsistent with their beliefs), but also the pope, who initially supported Galileo. Indeed, the Jesuits used everything in their arsenal—persuasion, deceit, diplomacy—to prevent Galileo from spreading his views. The result was that after 1650, the year the Church re-imposed a rigid orthodoxy, Italian science died (and much art died along with it). It wasn't until the late eighteenth century, when diverse commercial interests had regained power that both art and science were resurrected. And in 1979—almost 350 years after Galileo's condemnation—Pope John Paul II finally declared that the Catholic Church might have been mistaken in its condemnation, and he established a commission to study the case. Wouldn't the money have been better spent helping a Mother Teresa than on Rome-based Vatican bureaucrats?

The link between political power and science has been evident in China too. The inventiveness of the Chinese bloomed when the country was free of a rigid ideology. The three big innovations that brought about the Renaissance in Europe—the printing press, the compass, and gunpowder—all originated in China centuries before. But when rigid Confucianism was imposed during the Ming and Manchu dynasties, Chinese inventiveness ceased. This is a common scenario whenever state power increases. In China, becoming a government official was the only avenue of social mobility open to the ambitious and talented poor. They would have been foolish to promote ideas that could have threatened their only way to material well-being. Whether or not these socially mobile officials believed sincerely in the teachings of Confucius is a marginal issue. Acts are far more important than motives, and it is the conformists who survive. Meanwhile, much that passes for science in society isn't. Errors persist unchallenged. Joseph Needham, in *Science and Civilization in China,* his magisterial work on Chinese history, shows how when he writes:

> We must consider for a moment the five-element theories from the more practical point of view as a help or hindrance to the advance of the natural sciences. . . . Anyone who is tempted to mock at the persistence of it [in China] should remember that the founding fathers of the Royal Society spent much of their valuable time in deadly combat with the stout upholders of the four-element theory of Aristotle, and other "peripatetic fancies." . . . The only trouble about the Chinese five-element theories was that they went on too long. What was quite advanced for

the first century was tolerable in the 11th, and did not become scandalous until the eighteenth.

Sir Francis Bacon, in his *Advancement in Learning,* comments on the persistence in error of European schoolmen, to whom Needham alludes in the previous description. Bacon reflects accurately much of what is happening in today's academic market of ideas when he states:

> This kind of degenerate learning did chiefly reign among the schoolmen; who, having sharp and strong wits, and abundance of leisure, and small variety of reading (their wits being shut up in the cells of a few authors, chiefly Aristotle their Dictator, as their persons were shut up in the cells of monasteries and colleges), and knowing little history, either of Nature or Time, did, out of no great quantity of matter, and infinite agitation of wit, spin unto us those laborious webs of learning, which are extant in their books. For the wit and mind of man, if it work upon matter, which is the contemplation of the creatures of God, worketh according to the stuff, and is limited thereby; but if it work upon itself, as the spider worketh his web, then it is endless, and brings forth indeed cobwebs of learning, admirable for the fineness of thread and work, but of neither substance nor profit.

From these observations, Bacon reaches the conclusion that science should be made accessible to outsiders, and that it should influence people in a general way but not be used to build up disciples and research schools.

Indeed, there is considerable evidence that "fanatical" innovators could pursue their ventures and prevent a society's persistence in error if—and only if—they had access to outside, non-academic, non-governmental seed money. Needham makes this same point when he concludes that "a mercantile culture was able to do what agrarian bureaucratic civilization could not—bring to fusion point the formerly separated disciplines of mathematics and nature—knowledge." Unfortunately, Needham does not address why mercantile interests have such a powerful effect. But the reason is simple: mercantile interests are diverse, not dogmatic, and thus innovators have access to more than one source of finance.

SCIENCE AND THE DEMOCRATIZATION OF CAPITAL

The fewer the sources of finance, the fewer the innovations in all spheres of life, especially science. More democratized capital markets bring about more innovations. This has proved true through the ages.

For twenty-five years following the French Revolution, science flourished in France. In chemistry, astronomy, and mathematics, the French were the undisputed leaders. But science became centralized more quickly in France than it did in England, and centralization meant that a small group of scientists came to exercise power and patronage in Paris. Heresies developed in Britain, meanwhile, where diverse scientific experiments were financed from more diverse sources.

But the German universities were the ones that served during the nineteenth and early twentieth centuries as model academic institutions (though by the end of the nineteenth century their vitality had diminished). The initial rise happened at the same time that German cultural expansion spread over most of Central Europe. Central national universities, like those in Paris and Oxford-Cambridge, did not materialize. Innovations were more easily introduced, since the universities were on the peripheries, in perpetual rivalry, and had access to funding from various sources.

The eventual decline of the German universities began when they came to depend on the whimsical support of a few members of the ruling class, rather than sticking with the diversified business class. When academics rejected the demands of the business class for an increase in the number of chairs, and also balked at granting academic standing to new, practical subjects, the decline of the scientific enterprise began in earnest.

In France, and to varying extents in the rest of Europe, there is still too much control from the top, with politicians and bureaucrats deciding who gets grants for scientific work. The effect of this is best captured by James Gleick in his book *Chaos,* where he describes what has happened in France in the field of applied mathematics:

> Bourbaki succeeded as his founders could not have imagined. [Applied mathematics'] precepts, style, and notation became mandatory. It achieved the unassailable rightness that comes from controlling all the best students and producing a steady flow of successful mathematics. Its dominance over the École Normale was total and to [Benoit] Mandelbrot [a father of fractals, chaos theory, and much of today's applied mathematics], unbearable. He fled Normale because of Bourbaki, and a decade later he fled France for the same reason, taking up residence in the United States. Within a few decades, the relentless abstraction of Bourbaki would begin to die of shock brought on by the computer. . . . But that was too late for Mandelbrot, unable to live with Bourbaki's formalism and unwilling to abandon his geometrical intuition.\

Similar situations are all too common in Japanese universities too. An *Economist* article titled "No Ideas, Thanks, We're Academics" describes the circumstances in these words:

> Japanese universities are one of the strictest members-only parts of clubbish Japan. An academic career is organized around a *koza,* a chair. The chair is really a team consisting of a full professor, an associate professor and a few assistants. Its job is to carry out the full professor's research. Young academics are expected to do the legwork and help out with teaching undergraduates; they do not carry out research of their own. . . . Professors pick the best undergraduates to join their *koza.* . . . They get lifetime appointments within a couple of years, and are thereafter promoted by strict seniority. (Hence the outrage over Mr. Nichibe's [a professor at Tokyo University, Japan's Oxford] attempt to bring in an assistant professor who had not worked his way up through the pro-

162

fessor's *koza*.) Ten years at each level is common, with a professorship hovering in the mid-40s. That brings with it a place on the most powerful institution in any Japanese university, the board of professors, which alone can appoint new professors and so re-start the dismal promotional cycle.

The result has been that Japanese universities are, by international standards, backwaters. From 1901 to 1985, Japan won only five Nobel Prizes in science. One of the winners, Professor Susumu Tonegawa, who was trained at Kyoto University, won his prize in medicine for work done in Europe and America. He said that he could not have done the work if he had stayed inside the stifling Japanese university system.

This brief summary—and I did not even offer other well-known examples from the former Communist countries—shows that abstract scientific principles cannot prevent persistence in error, even in the natural sciences in societies where government is the sole source of finance. When this is the case, however, and the issue is validating political philosophies to fit rulers or governments, the social "sciences" become a real shambles.

THE SCIENCE OF POLITICAL LIES

Hegel's obscurity is well known. Scientists of his day (the early 1800s) did not take him seriously. And even his fellow philosopher Schopenhauer, quoting Shakespeare, once described his philosophy as "such stuff as madmen tongue and brain not."

What, then, was the source of Hegel's initial power and his lasting reputation? His philosophy espouses the advantages of concentrating power in the hands of the State, and he promotes the idea that all learning should be subordinated to State interest, a concept that suited his employer, Kaiser Frederick William III. He was the one who, in Schopenhauer's words:

> installed [Hegel] from above . . . as the certified Great
> Philosopher. [But Hegel] was a flat-headed, insipid, nau-

163

THE FORCE OF FINANCE

seating, illiterate charlatan, who reached the pinnacle of audacity in scribbling together and dishing up the craziest mystifying nonsense. This nonsense has been noisily proclaimed as immortal wisdom by mercenary followers and readily accepted as such by all fools, who thus joined into as perfect a chorus of admiration as had ever been heard before. . . . Governments make of philosophy a means of serving their state interests, and scholars make of it a trade.

Sir Karl Popper, who brought attention to the role of the kaiser in promoting Hegel, noted that Schwegler, an admiring disciple of Hegel's, never disputed the facts surrounding the source of his teacher's influence, even if he disagreed with Schopenhauer's views of Hegel's philosophy. Schwegler recognized that "the fullness of [Hegel's] fame and activity . . . properly dates only from his call to Berlin in 1818. Here . . . he acquired, from his connections with the Prussian bureaucracy, political influence for himself as well as recognition of his system as the official philosophy; not always to the advantage of the inner freedom of his philosophy, or of its moral worth."

Let us jump more than a century now and see how what happened with Hegel was more or less repeated with the establishment of macroeconomics as a field of science.

In the 1930s, as we saw in chapters one and four, many prominent economists agreed with Keynes's suggestion that spending money on public works, even if it was just to pay people to dig "holes in the ground," was a proper, temporary solution to a troubled economy. In the Depression era, capital markets had been destroyed—inadvertently perhaps—by monetary, fiscal, and political blunders, and thus no institution other than the government had the ability to borrow and advance credit to finance projects. Economists agreed on the nature of the solutions, but not on the causes of the Depression or Keynes's obscure definitions and generalized theories. They objected to his elitist suggestion that depressions would occur regularly in decentralized economies unless political wisdom, based (naturally) on the theories of economists like him, prevented them.

Keynes's ideas, not surprisingly, appealed to both politicians seeking to expand their power and economists seeking to establish power. Soon, Keynes's many followers had formed a sect. This is not to imply, however, as Schopenhauer did about Hegel, that Keynesians were charlatans, but is merely evidence of the fact that people respond to incentives. I have no doubt that many economists eventually became sincere Keynesians. But how did they convince people that his vague ideas were "science"?

In 1932, the U.S. Senate decided that information about the national income should be prepared for the years 1929–31, and Simon Kuznets was assigned the task. In 1941, he published the book *National Income and Its Composition, 1919–1938*. However, in his later writings he became critical of the thoughtless repetition of the computations in his early work.

Meanwhile, Milton Gilbert, head of the national income division of the U.S. Department of Commerce and a man strongly influenced by Keynes's ideas, began advocating the use of national income measures to examine relationships between defense expenditures and total output. Gilbert was unaffected by both Kuznets's criticism during the 1950s and that of Oscar Morgenstern (a father of "game theory") during the 1960s, although both men raised practical and conceptual concerns about the reliability of the numbers.

The use of aggregate statistics gained much legitimacy in 1953, with the publication of *A System of National Accounts and Supporting Tables by the Statistical Office of the United Nations*. Kuznets explicitly warned about the danger of using uniform methods of calculation for all countries, as well as the difficulties of interpreting such aggregate data in developing countries, but the United Nations proclaimed their "outstanding use . . . in connection with public policy."

The illusion of macroeconomics as a science had been achieved. There was "hard," neutral, positive-sounding numerical evidence to support it. Statistical tests could be run to determine the relationship between undefined and unreliable measures of consumption and savings and undefined and unreliable measures of "national product." It hardly mattered that no theory ever disproved anything, since using statistical methods on unreliable and undefined national aggregates and obscure jargon would always yield some kind of answer. There wasn't even any evidence in Keynes's own writings to justify the scientific ardor of his followers. In fact, if they had been able to put aside their political prejudices, economists would have noticed what Don Patinkin, an economic historian, eventually pointed out: that Keynes manufactured even the trivial evidence that appeared in his *General Theory*.

So what were the problems with using national aggregates? They ignored the fact that in one country they measured something that people wanted, while elsewhere they measured things that rulers and the establishment wanted (pork-barrel spending, in a best-case scenario, and torture chambers, prisons, and a powerful military, in the worst case). A fundamental component of aggregate counting—the strong assumption that the relationship between governments and citizens is based on an exchange of services backed by a maze of complex institutions to ensure accountability—was forgotten. Macroeconomic models summarized the working of the economy in a few simple-minded equations, and the conclusions were the same whether "production" and "output" were measured in countries with plenty of checks and balances or those with none.

By adding government "output" to whatever was produced in the "private" sector (though without ever raising any questions about what "private" means when capital markets are closed), economists transformed a self-serving political idea (a benevolent big government) into a neutral-sounding scientific debate about numbers and statistical methods. Macroeconomics thus became an obscure theory that could be taught in dictatorial regimes as well as democratic ones. The students became teachers, and macroeconomics and the illusion of objective national aggregates became a myth that governments, bureaucracies, and international agencies had an incentive to sustain and promote. But once people grow accustomed to obscurity, they become blind to the truth—words bias thoughts, after all—or perhaps they create their own blindness. Here is how the latter happens.

THE BLINDNESS OF FOLLOWERS

Most of us know the famous story of the Piltdown man hoax of 1912, when someone planted bones from a chimpanzee's jaw and a modern human's skull in an English gravel pit. The bones were dug up and widely hailed as having come from a prehistoric man. The finding fitted perfectly the traditional speculation in this field, which was that evolution modified the body piecemeal rather than as a whole. Thus a creature with a large human cranium and an apelike jaw was no surprise. In this case, a pre-existing belief blinded scientists to the reality of the situation. The hoax was not exposed for forty years.

The story of René Blondlot, a well-known French physicist from the early 1900s, is another case in point. Blondlot claimed to have discovered N-rays not long after Wilhelm Roentgen discovered X-rays. It was a time for new discoveries, and the French government, in particular, was anxious to find them in *France*. Science was a matter of national honor, but that honor was blemished by the perception that French scientists were no longer as innovative as their German and English counterparts. When Blondlot announced his "discovery," many competent French physicists were only too happy to confirm his findings. The hoax wasn't revealed until an American physicist, N. R. Wood, came to his laboratory and proved that the rays were nothing but an illusion. Whether Blondlot was blind or only pretended to be is irrelevant. Deeds matter; motives do not.

These two stories show that exposure to just one viewpoint makes it difficult—sometimes even impossible—for scientists to see the facts before their very eyes. One could argue, of course, that scientists have a duty to be prudent when considering new discoveries that contradict long-held beliefs. But such prudence must be balanced with open-mindedness, especially when the facts belie the established theories. For generations, however, scientists have all too often ignored the facts in favor of achieving or maintaining monopoly power.

Galileo's telescope was denounced as an instrument of the devil, and he was accused of trying to delude mankind. Orthodox astronomers refused to look through the glass, believing that men had invented the telescope to create the illusion of moons near Jupiter. Two hundred years later, physiologists refused to look through Hermann Helmholtz's ophthalmoscope, claiming that it was too dangerous to admit light into a diseased eye, and that the mirror he'd used would be of service only to occultists with defective eyesight.

Ignaz Semmelweis, the father of modern surgical sterilization techniques, committed suicide in 1865, two weeks after he was forcibly restrained in a sanatorium. Seventeen years earlier, in 1848, he had discovered, while working in a clinic, that if a physician washed his hands in a chlorine solution before delivering a baby, the maternal death rate dropped from 18 percent to one percent. Such a spectacular discovery should have led to a change in medical practices. It did not. In 1860, in the same clinic, 35 of 101 mothers died during childbirth. Semmelweis was perceived as an outsider, and thus was little more than a voice in the wilderness.

Sterilization was not adopted for another twenty years, when Joseph Lister and Louis Pasteur came along. Yet even then, their theories were not accepted without exhausting public debates. Envy, malice, and hatred were the order of the day, not scientific truth. René Valley-Radot, in *The Life of Pasteur*, writes that his "discoveries on ferments, . . . on microbes, the cause of contagious diseases, and the vaccination of those diseases, have been for biological chemistry, for the veterinary art and for medicine, not a regular process, but a complete revolution. Now, revolutions, even those imposed by a scientific demonstration, still leave vanquished ones behind who do not easily forgive. Therefore, Mr. Pasteur has many adversaries in the world without counting those Athenian French who do not like to see one man always right, or always fortunate." The masks of envy are many.

And the examples, sadly, don't end there. French mathematicians refused even to consider Benoit Mandelbrot's new language and computer-based approach, and his theory of applied fractal geometry was widely scorned. Michael Faraday encountered similar opposition when he announced his early discoveries in the field of electromagnetism. Few mathematical physicists gave them any attention, and indeed he was regarded as just more proof of the mathematical incapacity of the British.

Enforcing Blindness

To better understand how followers are taught to be "blind," consider for a moment a field far removed from sciences and university life—literature in sixteenth-century France.

Lucien Fèbvre describes the reaction other writers had to Rabelais's innovative books *Gargantua* and *Pantagruel*. They accused Rabelais of atheism and anti-Christian thought, all while flattering each other ("blurbs" by friends have an ancient history) and signaling students to follow in their footsteps. To encourage one young follower, Nicolas Bourbon, a leading critic of Rabelais, said, "Go, apply yourself to your work. No rest or respite till you have gained your place in the sun. Thus you will show yourself to be a man. Thus you will become another me." This same man called two collections of his writings *Nothings*—248 pages of nothings in 1533, 504 in 1538. Fèbvre notes that the title disturbed some of his colleagues, who asked what would happen if readers decided to take it literally? "It was a groundless fear," concludes Fèbvre. "There was no dishonor in writing nothings. It was only the turn of phrase that mattered, and the prosody."

Rabelais invented a number of new words that have since entered the French language and several others. But one, a word referring to the leading poets of his time, has been forgotten. It is the word "agelaste," which comes from Greek and means a man who does not laugh, who has no sense of humor. Rabelais detested and feared such men, and he complained that the "agelastes" treated him so atrociously that he nearly stopped writing. Language would not be ill-served if this word was reintroduced today.

Tom Wolfe's sarcastic description, in *From Bauhaus to Our House,* of events in the history of architecture in the twentieth century strikes a similar tone:

> Architects in a compound . . . which were now centered in
> universities . . . began to have the instincts of the medieval

clergy. The architect who insisted on going his own way stood no chance of being hailed as a pioneer of some important new direction. At best, he could hope to be regarded as an eccentric. . . . But what was supposed to be the source of a compound's authority? Why, the same as that of all new religious movements: direct access to the godhead. . . . So in the world of the architectural compounds, competition now took place on two levels. There was not merely the age-old competition to obtain commission and get the chance to show the world what you could do by designing buildings and seeing them go up. There was also the sheerly intellectual competition of the theories. . . . Thus there came into being another unique phenomenon: the famous architect who did little or no building.

This is no different from what has happened in economics and business schools; such schools are full of professors in finance, management, strategy, and so on who write about what companies should do, and how governments should regulate them, though they have never worked a day in either business or government. Until 1958, when the U.S. government started to heavily finance higher education (as we shall see in the next chapter), people became businessmen, financiers, or lawyers by practicing within companies, rather than by being taught by non-practitioners.

Words of ridicule and disdain for outsiders and words of praise for insiders are some of the methods used for teaching students to stick to orthodoxy. As Wolfe said, "The ambitious, young artist must join a 'movement,' a 'school,' an 'ism'—which is to say, a compound. He is either willing to join a clerisy and subscribe to its codes and theories or he gives up all hope of prestige." Praise provides the illusion of originality.

At the same time, truly new ideas, those requiring the use of a new vocabulary or the discarding of the orthodox one, are derided. In a recent book review of Joel Mokyr's *Lever of Riches,* David Landes, an economic historian from Harvard, makes a peculiar but revealing statement, one in line with both the aforementioned patterns and the comment by the *Wall Street Journal* reporter with which we started this chapter. Landes notes that an economist's use of the term "creativity," and his attempt to deal with the phenomenon, may alone be sufficient cause for his being disregarded by the profession.

IN PRAISE OF OBSCURITY

Many have noticed the propensity toward impenetrable jargon in the social sciences. Barbara Tuchman, the late historian, was among those who complained about it, and she warned her fellow historians to beware of those who have "painted themselves into a corner—or isolation ward—of unintelligibility. They know what they mean, but no one else does. Psychologists and sociologists are the farthest gone in the disease and probably incurable. Their condition may be pitied if one did not suspect it was deliberate. . . . No matter how illuminating their discoveries, if the behavioral scientists write only to be understood by one another, they must come to the end of the Mandarins."

But it is mathematical jargon, maybe more than any other, that makes even the most trivial subject look impressive, precise, and profound. This language has helped establish a hierarchy whose members, if forced to state clearly and in plain English what their models reveal about human behavior, would find themselves at a complete loss for words.

The obscurity of texts written by Saint-Simon, Hegel, Marx, Freud, Talcott Parsons, Keynes, and others has created opportunities for mediocre minds to make careers both within academia and outside it. There's a whole life to be made just from commenting on and interpreting the masters' vocabularies. This is not the place to examine their writings in any detail, but the *obscurity* of their writings is worthy of attention.

Sir Karl Popper, for instance, once remarked that Hegel's was a "scrutiny of thought so profound that it was for the most part unintelligible." Friedrich Hayek examined in detail Saint-Simon's confused, obscure writings, and was also known for his criticism of Keynes.

Robert Bork, in his *Tempting of America,* reached the same conclusion about obscurity in the field of constitutional law. He writes:

> To read the literature is to have one's worst fears confirmed. The sense that something in constitutional theory has gone awry begins with the style of argumentation. The older constitutional commentators, secure in their commonsense lawyers' view of the Constitution, wrote prose that remains clear, to the point, self-confident, and accessible to the nonprofessional reader. The modern theorists are different. Their concepts are abstruse, their sources philosophical, their arguments convoluted, and their prose necessarily complex. These writers are in fact undertaking . . . the alteration of the Constitution by "ingenious subtleties," "metaphysical refinements," and "visionary speculation" to make it not a document "addressed to the common sense of the people" but one addressed to a specialized and sophisticated clerisy of judicial power. . . . It is not, in truth, scholarship; it is, as one of its leading practitioners candidly states, the advocacy of political results addressed to courts.

Bork concludes that the very obscurity and inaccessibility of such views was, paradoxically, a source of their influence. This is because "the public at large and the legal profession as a whole are unaware of what is being taught and written, [and so] the reaction of ridicule and hostility that might have been expected has not been forthcoming. . . . [But] the message arrives where it counts. Because it is in effect coded, it is not read by outsiders."

It's not difficult to see, then, how, with governments massively financing the expansion of universities, politically motivated, linguistic obscurity takes over. The combination of obscurity and the illusion of devotion to "scientific" principles leads to an increasing hostility toward new ideas, and thus helps enforce the status quo not only within universities, but also outside them. The remedies to this situation are tackled in the next chapter.

CHAPTER 8

THE FUTURE OF HIGHER EDUCATION

If we think back over the past two decades, we can easily compile a list of the major industries that saw significant innovations (lowered prices, provision of better services, and rapid expansion). These include telecommunications, courier services, financial management, waste management, gambling, and so forth. These industries, disparate as they are, have something in common: they were all heavily regulated before they flourished. Their expansion came when government weakened its hold on them. The state governments in the United States no longer prohibited gambling, for example. MCI contested AT&T's monopoly in the courts and won. Federal Express filled the void left by the low-quality services provided by a government-protected postal monopoly. Local governments bungled waste management, opening opportunities in that area. And we could go on. In all these cases, the initial interference of government led to high prices (or taxes), low quality, or a combination of the two, creating many of the business opportunities of the past few decades.

Education—higher education, in particular—has not been an exception to this rule. The quality of education has been going down at all levels. If we do not see competition emerging in this area, it is only because governments still significantly regulate and subsidize the education business, both directly and indirectly. Moreover, many university administrators and academics oppose drastic internal restructuring—often at the same time that they preach it to businesses and governments. But these universities are in for a nasty surprise. They will fall into oblivion, and judging by their rigid adherence to the status quo the fall will come much more quickly than they seem to expect.

The problems universities face today, especially the decline in the reputation of scholars and scholarship, can be traced back to government interventions in this sector. These problems will be solved when governments do two things: lower taxes (leading students to expect higher after-tax incomes with which they can repay the tuition fees of the new, private businesses of higher learning) and cut subsidies to universities (allowing a private sector to emerge). Though politicians often frighten voters by saying that privatization of this sector would result in annual tuitions in the range of $30,000, that is simply false. Even in the United States, fewer than one percent of students pay this fee, and truly private universities have fees only in the $5,000 range. Nor is it true that the education of our young people will be negatively affected by privatization. On the contrary, it will have beneficial effects, even if it leads to the closing of maybe a third of today's North American universities. The privatization of the education business will also have the effect of diminishing the spread and persistence of false ideas, not only because of reasons explained in the previous chapter, but also because there will be fewer employment opportunities for retired politicians—a common, contaminating practice in today's universities.

WHY THE UNIVERSITY OF THE NEAR FUTURE
WILL BE DIFFERENT

Many universities have already made adaptations during the past two decades. To offset government cutbacks, the University of California, for example, slashed $900 million from its budget between 1989 and 1993. Other American universities eliminated entire departments—and their tenured professors.

Meanwhile, some private universities, including Harvard and Carnegie Mellon, used the Internet and video-conferencing to bring their courses to students around the world. These new technologies allow people direct and easy access to the experts, without filtering their knowledge through academic middlemen. The technology was combined with other changes. Today faculty, students, and businesses are all far more mobile, which also allows easier direct interaction. Moreover, geographic attachments play a diminished role. In the past, local businesses subsidized local universities because they expected to benefit from both the students and the research staff. Technology and more open borders have changed that, too. Businesses can now be in easy, permanent contact with research facilities around the world. And the chances that students will stay in the same region (or even the same country) after they graduate have diminished too. Why, taxpayers wonder, should they invest in local universities and local students if they themselves use the services of institutions elsewhere in the world and the students are likely to end up paying taxes in other countries?

At the same time, these technological and political changes have brought about rapid obsolescence of skills. Many more people are expected to return to classrooms to upgrade or even change their skill sets. This means that institutions of higher learning will have to adapt to a student body that is older, more experienced, and more concerned with upgrading skills than with obtaining pieces of paper called degrees or having access to nice campuses and winning athletic teams. This will impose stricter constraints on today's academics—a topic we'll examine later in this chapter.

All these changes lead us to one inevitable conclusion: the question is no longer whether to retract, consolidate, restructure, and adapt universities, but whether these reforms can be accomplished from within or will be imposed from without. Given the situation at most universities today—and this is typical of most businesses too—it seems likely that outside pressures will force changes on them.

The pressures for change—in families, businesses, governments, non-profit organizations, and so on—begin with either tight money or expectations of tight money because of competition and reduced subsidies. Both conditions affect institutions of higher education today. Because of today's drastic technological, financial, and political changes, universities of tomorrow will have to rely on higher tuition fees, to be sure, though far below the $20,000 to $30,000 range, as noted above. The DeVry Institutes (a Chicago-headquartered private university, whose stock is traded on the NASDAQ), with their twenty-four thousand students on eleven campuses in the U.S. and Canada, charge $5,600 a year for an MBA, and a similar yearly tuition for students taking degrees in electronics, data processing, and accounting. Other new, rapidly expanding private universities charge fees in a similar range.

UNIVERSITIES COMMERCIALIZING THE NEW TECHNOLOGIES: PRESSURES FROM OUTSIDE

Since it was established nearly twenty years ago, the University of Phoenix has become one of the largest private accredited business schools in the U.S. The university has focused exclusively on the professional education of the working adult student. The governing body, including the board of directors, has been relentless in its pursuit of practical, results-oriented curricula.

With the introduction in 1989 of its online program, the university made its business programs available to a population of working adults whose choices had primarily been limited to the isolation of correspondence studies. By 1993, one thousand students were enrolled in this program.

Once they're registered, students are sent textbooks, a course guide, and the special menu-driven software that allows them to "go" to the virtual classroom. Students have electronic access to the library, technical assistance, and financial aid. The courses are convenient not only because they can be taken at any time, but also because students can start during any month of the year. There is no problem with matching schedules.

How does it work? Students are grouped with a faculty member in small classes of ten to fifteen people. Discussions are held, assignments given, and feedback provided, all in a classroom that is attended electronically rather than physically. At the beginning of each course, students receive a comprehensive syllabus, with assignments and dates for the entire class. At the end of every week, the instructors let each student know how he or she did during that week.

In contrast to correspondence courses, the online classroom is highly structured. Students must keep up with their classes and meet weekly deadlines. The frequent discussions and assignments mean that a student must electronically visit her classroom at least five days out of every week. To maintain control over the quality of its courses, Phoenix supervises the content, designs the course, and then hires somebody competent—that is, a person with experience in the field—to deliver it. The university becomes, essentially, an information broker.

Phoenix developed many of its courses in response to demands from the business community, and many of the instructors work full- time during the day in the industries about which they teach. There is no tenure; the professors are freelancers, which has not led to lowered standards. The university is accredited by the same institution that accredits the University of Chicago, the University of California, and many other established universities around the U.S. It also has alliances with major corporations such as U.S. West Inc. and Intel, and provides customized training programs for employees of these companies. Employers pay the tuition of about 80 percent of Phoenix's students. The university now has campuses in New Mexico, Utah, Colorado, Nevada, and Hawaii, and it has contracts to set up and market adult education—especially online education—for fourteen private colleges. It is also a private, for-profit business—and a successful one. Its parent group is Apollo Group Inc., which also owns an adult-education consulting company and an in-house publisher. In 1995, it became a public company, with a market valuation of US$2.3 billion in June 2000.

How do students perform in these online courses? A study followed the results of identical undergraduate and graduate courses online and in person over three years. The only course where there were significant differences in the performance of the two groups was one in computer science. The online students did better. The research also found that studying online has encouraged collaboration among students. This is not surprising, since the barriers preventing students from getting together diminish. This happens not only because geographical distance is no longer an issue, but also because the new technologies overcome prejudice and personal challenges such as physical impairments, hearing impairments, and speech impediments. Shyness and timidity are no longer issues, either.

The research also found that the roles of both students and professors change. The professor becomes a facilitator, a coordinator who puts together a set of resources and then guides the students through the course. To put it simply: the technology allows knowledge to be democratized.

Let us examine a few additional numbers and developments. In 1986, a consortium of engineering schools called the National Technical University, in collaboration with fourteen corporations, began sending course lectures via satellite to other universities and to workplaces. In 1995, forty-five universities, including MIT, Cornell, Purdue, and the University of California at Berkeley, joined in, offering engineering courses to four hundred corporations, including several defense contractors in the Washington area. Companies can upgrade their employees' skills without incurring the costs of sending them away. Carnegie Mellon is now collaborating with McGraw-Hill, Sony, and Bell Atlantic, and will soon offer a range of courses beamed from Pittsburgh to Asia and Europe.

The chairman and founder of Phoenix University, John G. Sperling, said it was the inflexibility of college programs that led him to start his venture twenty years ago. Corporations also grew dissatisfied with the content and rigidity of many programs during the past decade. As a result, Texas Instruments established a virtual university. And like numerous large European corporations, Motorola and DuPont have their own universities. While the academics who teach for these corporations have no tenure, they earn about double the salary they can get at ordinary universities.

Sperling also anticipated the shift in the student body. In 1970, those twenty-five or older made up only 27 percent of U.S. college enrolment. By 1991, this figure had grown to 45 percent. Ordinary universities were slow to respond to the flexibility in both time and place that these new customers required, but Phoenix's online service had no trouble accommodating this demographic shift.

In Europe, too, universities became more entrepreneurial as government coffers emptied during the past decade. In England, Cambridge University has established a science park, an attempt to bring a little Silicon Valley–type entrepreneurship to its campus. Other English universities have shifted their fund-raising energies from non-profit endeavours to for-profit ones. Both the London School of Economics and Warwick University have set up private companies to sell their research. Warwick now gets more than half its income from non-governmental sources, and it regards its private income as more reliable than the traditional government sources.

Still, it should be stressed that the new technology is no panacea in the education business. Oral communication skills cannot be developed electronically, and debating through electronic media is more time-consuming and less effective. And such universities cannot replicate the college experience that youngsters expect today. Many students go to university not necessarily because they want to learn, but because there are other young people there. It is also true that some younger people need the discipline and the motivation that only personal interactions can bring forth. For them, the online universities are not a solution.

However, the emerging trends suggest that young people will soon be able to choose the combination of services and learning they want. Some universities will offer only skills upgrading, while others will offer a certain lifestyle. Students who want to finish their studies quickly, or study only part-time, will chose the former option. They will be unwilling to pay for a university whose fees also cover athletic teams and ivy-covered buildings. There is no reason for all universities to bundle learning with sports and a nice campus, and ask students to bear the cost. The present relative uniformity of higher education is due to the fact that government is the main financial intermediary in this sector.

What is preventing most Canadian, American, and European universities from adapting more quickly? Why are there already some 1,400 corporations venturing into the "university business" under their own corporate umbrella? Two interest groups are standing in the way of these changes: mediocre and worse-than-mediocre professors, and mediocre and worse-than-mediocre students. To understand the obstacles these two groups represent, we must first explore how they were created.

HOW DID UNIVERSITIES GET INTO THEIR PRESENT SHAPE?

In the 1950s, a few extraordinary events shaped the business of higher education in the U.S. and brought it to its present form, a form then emulated in other countries. One event was the launching of the Sputnik satellite in 1957. With this, education became associated with the military and the need to catch up. The Soviets' apparent lead in the technology race seemed to many in the U.S. to be a result of deficiencies in the American education system. Because of this, the federal government launched a major program of support for education in 1958, under the National *Defense* Education Act. The following numbers give a rough indication of the effect of this sudden massive increase in financing. Between 1960 and 1983, undergraduate enrollment trebled, growing from 3,227,000 to 9,707,000. The greatest increases occurred in state schools of the second rank and two-year colleges. In 1960, schools with two-year programs had accounted for only 14 percent of all enrollments, but by 1982 such institutions played host to 42 percent of all undergraduate students. In 1962, professors were relatively young (with 44 percent in their twenties or thirties). By 1981, fewer than a quarter were younger than forty.

The second item that shaped the business of higher learning was the civil rights movement. Pieces of legislation such as the GI Bill implied that it was a wise investment to make it easier for "average" Americans to go to college. The correct inference should only have been that access to credit was a good thing. It's never true that by subsidizing "averages," governments can improve the situation of everyone in society. When averages get subsidized, averages also get taxed. And of course, the brighter members of society will get more out of subsidized education, thus bills such as the GI Bill actually have the effect of increasing inequality. A smart eighteen-year-old, for example, may end up with a $100,000 subsidy today, but a kid not as smart, or one who has been denied the opportunity for decent schooling the whole way along, will not get that amount to open a gas station or a corner store, and thus he stays poor. People then blame "society" for the increased inequality.

The third event that helped shape U.S. universities was the baby boom. Demographic changes are not destiny, but they help explain many changes. The extraordinary cohort that first entered the world nine months after VJ day hit college age during the 1960s. To keep up with the sudden increase in the student body, governments started to heavily subsidize universities, and universities began expanding their staffs. One unexpected result of the sudden expansion was that many people were hired merely to fill voids, not because they had any particular interest in (or facility for) teaching. This eventually led to a slow, continuous decline in the vitality of universities. In 1963, Aldous Huxley predicted the ruinous effects on science of such sudden expansion when he wrote:

> Let us face the facts. A large number of young people
> take up scientific research as a career these days, but

regrettably few are impelled into it by a passionate curiosity as to the secrets of nature. For the vast majority it is a job like any other job. . . . Moreover, it is not generally realized outside of the academic circles how far a mediocre research worker can get. . . . In commerce and industry there are those who are exceptionally endowed with brilliance, ruthlessness or luck and achieve proportionate success; then come the vast majority who somehow manage to get through, and the minority who go under. The proportion of scientists who go under is probably much lower and the weeding process is correspondingly less effective. Indeed, the relative security and stability of the research career are probably more attractive to mediocrities than the romance of inquiry to the brilliant ones.

Academic staffs could not have been expanded without the subsidies governments provided. These subsidies exacerbated the decline by keeping fees low, thus inducing universities to accept an increasing number of students. Let's see now how the subsidies have also led to a decline in what passes for scholarship and teaching, while at the same time creating powerful interest groups of, at best, mediocre professors and mediocre students.

MIRAGES OF SCIENCE

When a producer—any producer—wants to sell a product but has no buyers, he or she can do one of three things: decide to do something else, persist and go bankrupt, or search for additional credit and try to find the product's market. Banks and legal institutions help determine the outcome. For companies whose shares are traded on the stock market, fluctuations in price give an indication of people's confidence in the viability of the enterprise. Even if a company has no revenue whatsoever, it can still secure credit if people expect successful commercialization in the future.

These arrangements prevent companies from persisting in error for too long—unless governments interfere. Once they do, the picture changes. When governments subsidize an industry, directly or indirectly (by preventing a competitor's entry, for example), businesses can persist even if others could have offered better services and at less than the non-subsidized price. With governments acting as financial intermediaries, "markets" can thus "persist in error," offer inferior products, and even pay pliable consultants to come up with theories to rationalize the government's intervention (in the name of "national interest," for example).

This is what has happened with the "scientific enterprise" at universities in recent years. Since most members of the expanded academic staffs at the suddenly vastly expanded universities had little to say yet were required to produce "original research" to get tenure, they responded by inventing new vocabularies. The result was an explosion of endless theories written in jargon that was getting more obscure by the day. To paraphrase Willa Cather: Give the people a new word and they think they have a new fact. The professors gave the vastly expanded student body many new (subsidized) words, eventually creating the cacophony that today passes for social science and for research in the humanities. Since at that time, most university professors still enjoyed a vaunted reputation, one can forgive people for falling prey to the confusion Cather alludes to—for a while.

To prove that this is no exaggeration, let's look briefly at a sampling of the style and content of what passes for scholarly research in the social sciences and humanities today. In a recent issue of the *American Sociological Review,* we find the following typical passage:

> In effect, it was hypothesized that certain physical data categories, including housing types and densities, land use characteristics, and ecological location, constitute a scalable content area. This could be called a continuum of residential desirabilities. Likewise, it was hypothesized that several social strata categories, describing the same census

tracts, and referring generally to the social stratification system of the city, would also be scalable. This scale could be called a continuum of socio-economic status. Thirdly, it was hypothesized that there would be a high positive correlation between the scale types of each continuum.

In translation, this means that richer people live in nicer neighborhoods and in bigger houses. But the *American Sociological Review* is by no means alone. In a recent issue of the *Communication Quarterly*, a ten-page article presents the view that music video programs boost the sales of pop music recordings—and cites forty-three other scholarly articles to make the point. Such trivialities are counted as advancements in knowledge, and they are the basis on which professors ask for government funding to subsidize research. These are also the texts that give tenure, become required reading, and teach our present generation of students what constitutes research.

Even in the prestigious journal *PMLA* (Publications of the Modern Language Association), the style is no different. Here is a quote that is typical of the language used by members of this association:

> We have now come to see, however, that the partitioning of art and history derives from a false dichotomy. Historical awareness is a construing of records already encoded, which can only be interpreted according to a historical poetics. And fictive ideologies are the stuff of history, which must be comprehended by linguistic and dramatistic analysis. All cultural phenomena are artifacts, at once real and fictive. The binocular perspective enables us to restore enacted courtesy, courtesy as lived, to the realm of poetic performance and to consider anew what such a way of living would have been like.

More than a century ago, the English social critic John Ruskin put this passage in two simple sentences: "Great nations write their autobiographies in three manuscripts, the book of their deeds, the book of their words and the book of their art. Not one of these books can be understood unless we read the two others."

At the Modern Language Association's 1991 annual meeting, the papers presented included "The Detective as Pervert," "Of AIDS, Cyborgs and Other Indiscretions: Inscribing Morphologies of the Body in the Postmodern," "Strategies of Teaching a Feminist Political Latin American Culture Course," "The Polygenesis of Long Vowels in North Italian Dialects: An Autosegmental Analysis," "The Lesbian Phallus: Or, Does Heterosexuality Exist?" "The Rhetoric of Disaster: Rhetorical Analysis of Technical Discourse in Congressional Oversight Hearings," "Self-Consuming Fictions: The Dialectics of Cannibalism in Recent Caribbean Narratives," "Gross Feeders and Flowing Cups: Is Naked Ministering Pornographic in Book 5 of *Paradise Lost?*" and "Telling It Slant: Personal Narrative and the Reality of Leprosy."

All these papers were written in the same unreadable style, making use of the language of obscurity we examined in chapter seven. And consider this passage from a recent book from Princeton University Press:

> It is also an argument for taking the variation in the periphery as a starting point for investigation and, more importantly, for examining the historical interaction of indigenous and foreign notions of political authority, structures of domination and mechanisms of appropriation as they combine to create the unprecedented circumstances and institutions of politics in the modern periphery.

Or here is a political scientist, David Held, discussing nautonomic structures (whatever they are) in a recent book, *Reinventing the Left:*"Nautonomic structures are shaped by the availability of a diverse range of socially patterned resources from the material (wealth and income) and the coercive (organized might and the development of force) to the cultural—the stock of concepts and discourses which mould interpretive frameworks, tastes and abilities." Is there anything that does not shape "nautonomic structures"?

And here is a gem from Dominique Laporte's history of human waste, *Histoire de la Merde,* published by MIT Press, no less: "The imperative of profit marks the return of a repressed fantasy of which utility is merely the displaced reversal, that is, the dream of satisfying all need and thus liberating the subject from lack. Hence the primordial status of philanthropy and hygiene alongside the supposed 'three sources' in the genealogy of Marxism." It does not make much more sense in the original French.

Even a best-seller like Allan Bloom's *The Closing of the American Mind* contains such language: "If openness means to 'go with the flow' it is necessarily an accommodation to the present. That present is so closed to doubt about so many things impeding the progress of its principles that unqualified openness to it would mean forgetting the despised alternatives to it, knowledge of which makes us aware of what is doubtful in it." The fact that Bloom's book was read so widely means that at least people are ready to give scholars another try.

Today there are about eighteen thousand "scholarly" journals, most of which are published in the U.S. When I was writing on this topic a few years ago, I checked a large sample of these journals. There were no significant differences between them as far as their style and content were concerned. They all pretended to present "innovative" theories, most without any regard for facts or any attempt to confront alternative explanations. How did this come to be standard practice not only in the social sciences and humanities, but also in law and business schools? And how is such obscure output linked with government subsidies and low tuition fees?

THE DETRIMENTAL EFFECTS OF
GOVERNMENT INTERVENTION

Academics who specialize in inventing and practicing obscure languages have fewer employment opportunities in private industry than those who are interested in practical subjects and in communicating their findings to a larger public. Thus these academics have a great incentive to insure their teaching careers, and they have far more invested in academic politics than those of their colleagues who actually have something to say.

Slowly, the academics specializing in obscurity have taken hold of the curriculum, organizing seminars and conferences, getting appointed to various committees, and even successfully promoting the view that a person is not worthy of the name "scholar" unless he writes obscurely for a highly specialized journal. If he is even understood by the non-professional reader, his scholarship is suspect.

This attitude is strange. The study of the liberal arts and of business is supposed to teach us to confront and debate difficult ideas in a calm and civilized way. It is supposed to encourage analysis rather than foment passions, and it teaches that a person who keeps his learning to himself or a small group of insiders has not gained any wisdom. The word "education" comes from the Latin *educere*, which means "to lead out." It matters very little what we know if we cannot communicate it and do not even take the trouble to try.

At first, those involved in research may have been interested in giving up some professional and administrative duties, since their interests lay elsewhere. By the time they noticed the increased power of their "scholarly" colleagues, it was too late. Their journal publications and work on committees and conferences were taken as evidence—by government bureaucrats—of their importance and expertise.

Soon, an alliance was struck between the scientifically unproductive (who organized conferences and raised funds) and the scientifically undistinguished (who gave speeches at these conferences and filled the subsidized publications). A government agency once made the mistake of asking me to evaluate whether its subsidies to a journal should continue. To answer this question, I looked at two things. One was whether the articles in this journal were ever quoted in any other journal. The answer in this case was no. The second thing I looked at was the ratio of articles published to articles submitted. It was 1:1. I obviously recommended the funding be discontinued, but today, almost ten years later, the journal still exists.

And there are new government funding options being offered all the time. In March 2000, for example, the Privy Council of Canada (which serves the prime minister and also supervises the Policy Research Secretariat) started sponsoring *Isuma: The Canadian Journal of Policy Research. Isuma* is published by the Presses de l'Université de Montréal—with no mention made anywhere that it is a politically monitored and paid publication with an editorial board composed of Ottawa bureaucrats.

All this brings into being not only a politicized academic tribe, but also a large graduated bureaucracy and a mediocre student body (which by now also depends on the continuing recognition of the new obscurities and politically motivated research). But what happens if a field falls into oblivion, the politicians leave office, or the "research" ceases to be taught at the university?

ESTABLISHING MYTHOLOGIES

Let's recall for a moment the cargo cults we examined in the first chapter. During the Second World War, the people of New Guinea saw airplanes filled with food and other good stuff literally descend out of the clear blue sky. When the planes eventually stopped coming, the New Guineans tried everything to get them back. They built runways, made headphones and antennas out of wood, constructed airplanes of sticks and leaves—and the priests of the tribe prayed. From a distance, their creations seemed perfect, completely real—just like many universities and fields of research seem today.

The entrenched attitudes call to mind a scene described by the writer Larry McMurtry, who was watching his novel *Horseman, Pass By* get turned into the movie *Hud,* with Paul Newman. There is a moment when Newman shoots at a buzzard on a tree and several others fly away. The problem for the film crew was how to keep the buzzards on the tree and prevent them from flying away too soon. They decided to wire their feet and release them after Newman fired. The buzzards didn't want to co-operate, however.

They tried to fly, but since the wire held them back, they just fell forward, flapping their wings. It turned out that the circulatory system of the buzzard doesn't work when it is upside down, and the buzzards in the film soon passed out. After this sequence repeated itself six times, however, the birds no longer pitched forward. Now the problem became that when the wire was released, they didn't fly away. They had learned from the experience that if they were to try to fly, they would faint.

The buzzard story is by no means unique. An experiment with monkeys gives us an even better lesson on the reverence paid to precedents.

Four monkeys were put in a room. In the center of the room, there was a tall pole with bananas suspended from the top. Whenever a monkey tried to retrieve them, however, he was hit with a shower of cold water. After several attempts yielded the same result, the monkeys stopped trying. At this stage, one of the original monkeys was removed and a new one was added. When the newcomer reached for the bananas, the other three pulled him back. After a few tries, the new monkey also got the message and stopped trying. One by one, the original monkeys were replaced, and each new monkey learned the same lesson: don't reach for the bananas. Though the new generation of monkeys had never received the cold shower, they adhered to this behavior.

What's the lesson? I don't want to suggest that academics are like buzzards or monkeys. What I am suggesting, however, is that precedents are incorporated into behavior and institutions, and often outlive the circumstances that created them. By now, there exist many tenured professors who have trained a new generation of students in their own specialized language of obscurity. Once these students get their Ph.D.s—frequently after six or more tedious years—they won't fly away or reach for forbidden fruits, but will adhere to the customs of the tribe. They know that invitations to conferences, publications in scholarly journals, and tenure all depend on their not deviating too much from the path. They thus become imprisoned in their words and habits.

The thing that prevents much of what passes for scholarship from being science, however, is exactly what prevents the cargo cults from waking up from their illusions: scientific honesty and a willingness to judge; the candor to report not only one's own views and findings, but also views that are in opposition; and a willingness to debate ideas, openly showing why and how certain conclusions were reached. Both the academics and the cargo cults refuse to make such confrontations.

But the experiment with the monkeys teaches us something more. The monkeys accepted the teachings of their peers because they were being fed. If they weren't, an entrepreneurial, hungry monkey would probably have started to reach for the bananas again. Does this have implications for today's tenure system—a system that comes with automatic salary increases? Take away the job security of this system and public universities would be transformed.

Let us look now at everything we've just discussed from an additional angle. In spite of the pretensions—and in spite of the endless emphasis on research and publications—the academic profession is essentially a teaching profession, not a scholarly one—and that is as it should be. The question is: Who decides on the content of this teaching?

Not surprisingly, the greatest shift in what was to be taught in undergraduate courses in the social sciences and humanities in the U.S. occurred during the 1960s. Preoccupations with graduate school took hold in many institutions, and soon undergraduate studies began reflecting the way the disciplines were conceived at the doctoral level. Faculty members started to spend much of their time discussing the work of their fellow professors, and they gave more attention to the narrow models of their discipline. Soon business schools, for example, were filled with faculty members who taught management and finance but had never actually solved a real-life managerial or financial problem. Imagine if this were allowed to happen in medical schools, with future physicians taught surgery by professors who had never performed an operation in their lives.

We should by no means confuse "science" with what university professors do. Such confusion leads to the unwarranted expectation that professors should be seriously involved in "research," not just teaching. Such expectations then create pressures that lead to the proliferation of foolish and trivial research *and* to a decline in the quality of teaching.

So from all of the above we can conclude the following:

- Science will not be adversely affected if government subsidies are cut.
- Teaching will not be adversely affected if subsidies are cut.
- While it's true that if tuitions are raised and entire departments closed, some students will no longer be able to attend university, it's equally true that these students should not have been subsidized to start with. The U.S. Bureau of Labor Statistics recently reported that about 20 percent of all college graduates work in fields that don't require any degree. Subsidized education has led only to expensive disappointments for both individuals and society, and a general lowering of standards at universities.
- It is not true that universities have fostered better understanding and mutual tolerance among individuals and groups. In fact, government financial intermediation has destroyed civil interactions and traditional discourse. To obtain subsidies for journals and conferences, academics had to show that they really had something different to say. The discussion had to be in black and white, rather than nuanced. The result has been that groups have the luxury of pursuing their activities in splendid isolation, within subsidized mutual-admiration societies.

The question now is how do we get from this dismal situation to a promising future—and do it by re-organizing universities from within, rather than waiting until they're organized from the outside.

A POSSIBLE SEQUENCE

In 1993, a group of sixteen business leaders, educators, and foundation executives published a document titled *An American*

191

Imperative: Higher Expectations for Higher Education. Its message was:

- that undergraduate education in the United States is too often "little more than secondary school material—warmed over and reoffered at much higher expense";
- that high schools lost relevance when they ceased to be held accountable for their kids' education, and that they expect colleges and universities to fill the gaps they've left; and
- that universities produce a surplus of "unskilled applicants scrambling to earn a precarious living," and that as a result there is "a disturbing and dangerous mismatch between what the United States needs of higher education and what it is getting."

Though the authors of the document discuss the problems, they don't examine how the universities (and the high schools, for that matter) managed to get into their present shape—in spite of the vast subsidies they receive—and they don't offer solutions. Let's see now how a greater reliance on private financing—and the increased accountability such reliance would engender—is one possible solution.

Students who pay $5,000 for four courses, expecting to be repaid from future income, have a good incentive to study hard, do well, and learn as much as they can. Equal opportunity will come when all people have access to loans, not low tuition fees. Students themselves are in the best position to evaluate their abilities and ambitions, and they can decide if they want to take the loans to study. There is one problem with this solution, of course, and that is taxes. If taxes are high and expected after-tax incomes low, students will not be able to pay high tuition fees. Governments, when they contemplate privatizing universities, must lower taxes first. The Mike Harris government in Ontario announced in October 2000 that it had cleared the way for private universities in that province. It is no accident that the announcement came after a few years of decreased taxes. The federal government is now moving in the same direction.

But how do private universities solve the problems we've already discussed? One obstacle to reforming the system has always been the lack of a financial commitment on the part of students. Students would be more engaged if they had a great deal at stake financially. The possibility that they would vote with their feet when dissatisfied would help establish and maintain higher standards of teaching and better administrative services. Students in different fields would pay different fees. There is no reason, for instance, for a medical student, an engineer, or a law student to pay the same fee as a student in philosophy or literature. And the fear of exorbitant tuition fees is misplaced. Once the system is deregulated—as happened with phone service, for example—prices will drop and people will be able to buy a variety of services at different prices.

And even if fees are moderately higher, that will probably only have the effect of sending people out to work for a few years before they complete their studies; others will pursue their education on a part-time basis. This also will help raise standards. Older, more experienced students will keep the professors on their toes, and many of the fields currently pretending to be sciences will dwindle away. Also, if the experienced, older students themselves decide to become social scientists, they will be able to make better judgments about human behavior than today's scholars, since they will have greater life experience.

The higher and differential tuition fees should also come together with financial arrangements allowing those students accepted to university to take out loans to pay for their studies. The money spent on universities, whether through loans or grants, should be channeled through the students (the customers), not the universities (the producers).

Before any of this can happen, however, taxes must be lowered. The sequence matters: we cannot increase tuition fees first and cut taxes later.

WHAT ELSE CAN BE DONE?

The last major transformation of the university in the West happened in 1876, when Daniel Gilman became the first president of Johns

Hopkins and decided to adopt the model of the University of Berlin. At that time, American colleges were mainly involved in the training of ministers, the propagation of religions, the teaching of the so-called learned professions, and the improvement of the moral character of young men. As the first great graduate school in the U.S., Johns Hopkins set a new standard for academic achievement, investing *not* in magnificent buildings but in magnificent faculty members. Harvard, Cornell, Michigan, and Columbia followed in quick succession.

Today no less a change is required. Electronic highways allow students to bypass local academic intermediaries and get to experts directly. The impact is similar to that of Gutenberg's printing press. That invention brought literacy to the masses, and it narrowed the distance between believer and priest, citizen and ruler, scholar and layman. Those who shunned the print revolution—the Muslim clergy in the Ottoman Empire, for example, who said it was blasphemy—doomed their people. In more open societies, the middlemen were the ones who were doomed.

People interested in learning can go around today's middlemen, get in contact with expert researchers, and gain direct experience from the best. Such contacts count for more than university degrees, which government subsidies and resulting institutional arrangements have turned into little more than pieces of paper.

As we saw in chapter one, many constitutions around the world also ended up as little more than pieces of paper once governments became major financial intermediaries, and for similar reasons. If we let our institutions of higher learning draw from diverse financial sources, the "business of knowledge" will be restructured. People will still invent mythologies, and fads will still exist. But they will be of shorter duration.

CHAPTER 9

A FINANCIAL
TWENTY-FIRST CENTURY

Prosperity requires people to abandon old industries and old ways of doing things, and bet on new ones and new ways. Money and people must move from yesterday's industries to those of the future, whether that move takes place in the same country or across borders. And any such move must be financed.

Of course, these moves are bets. Someone must decide how much money to bet, on whom, when, and where. When capital markets are open, so-called angels, venture capitalists, banks, investment banks, leveraged-buyout firms, and asset-management firms make these matches, betting on the vision of entrepreneurs and managers and holding them accountable. When capital markets are closed, governments, family members, and "criminal elements" decide on the matches. In those circumstances, some people vote with their feet, opting to move to countries with more open capital markets.

So what are we to think when we see claims, such as the one made by Jeffrey Sachs, a high-profile Harvard-based economist, in a recent issue of *The Economist,* that "free markets are not enough: successful innovation requires supporting institutions." What can be the meaning of this? Don't "free markets" already imply innovation and a maze of complex supporting institutions? Aren't such institutions necessary to create trust, enforce contracts, and preserve equality before the law? Sachs then states that some countries have been left behind in today's global economy because "we know that technology is less likely to converge than capital. Innovation shows increasing returns to scale, meaning that regions with advanced technologies are best placed to innovate further." These assertions are contradicted by facts.

What does it mean to say that technology converges less than capital? One possible answer is this: Some people know technology, have up-to-date skills, and innovate, while others do not. If those in the first group move from one country to another—Chinese mainlanders moving to Taiwan and Hong Kong, for example, or people moving from India to the Silicon Valley—they transfer technological know-how quickly, and technologies "converge." Technologies and innovations have little to do with geographic location. If they're denied opportunities in one place and given them elsewhere, people, especially traders and the better skilled, will move. This is why so many technologically advanced regions have fallen behind because of a brain drain. The places to which these "brains" moved flourished. And capital has always followed the brains. After all, where do we put our money, if not on critical masses of talent?

Robert Barro, Sachs's colleague, has made similar assertions. In one of his studies on growth, he states the following: "A key issue in economic development is whether economies that start out behind tend to grow faster in per capita terms and thereby converge toward those that began ahead." Why is this an issue at all when the facts have been known since antiquity? Here is what Herodotus wrote in book one of his *Histories* (that's 2,500 years ago): "For most cities which were great once are small today; and those which used to be small were great in my own time. Knowing, therefore, that human prosperity never abides long in the same place, I shall pay attention to both alike."

Societies leapfrogged one another not only in ancient Greece and Rome, but in many parts of the world ever since. Byzantium, Spain and Portugal, the Italian city-states, the Arab countries, the Ottoman Empire, the Netherlands, England, China, the South American countries (remember that during the inter-war period, Argentina was one of the richest countries in the world), Hong Kong, Singapore, Scotland, Taiwan, Palestine-turned-Israel—all rose, and some later declined, not only in relative terms, but in absolute ones too. Why, in this so-called information age, has this knowledge failed to reach economists? Perhaps there is too much noise in what passes for "information," and the proper questions are not being raised.

There isn't much more evidence to back Sachs's other assertion that "geographical conditions are important . . . to absorb technologies from abroad. Successful importers of technology tend to be close to big markets or on principal sea routes or both." What can he be referring to? Geography is not destiny, and never has been. Mexico has a wonderful location just south of the United States. It has never moved. Yet for centuries, it absorbed neither technology nor capital from its northern neighbor. Northern Mexico is changing today, to be sure, yet that's obviously not because geography has changed, but because internal politics have. There is a division between northern and southern Europe, but that isn't a matter of geography either. Geographically and politically isolated Israel has been prospering and attracting skilled people. Its neighbor Lebanon prospered as well (until politics put an end to its success), but other Middle Eastern nations did not. None of these triumphs and turmoils has anything to do with geography.

And there is more. Out-of-the-way Iceland, Australia, and New Zealand are all prosperous and technologically up to date. They are not close to either big markets or principal sea routes. What they do have in common, however, are relatively open capital markets and, in the latter two cases, migration. In short, what rapidly prospering nations over the past centuries have shared is the ability to attract skilled, entrepreneurial people to their shores. It is these people who quickly brought know-how to places that were previously isolated either by geography or—far more frequently—by politics.

But there is a link between location and prosperity. Contrary to Sachs's assertion, however, it has to do with politics, rather than geography. Rulers tended to build their capital cities away from trade routes, far from seaports. That's why we have Moscow and St. Petersburg, Barcelona and Madrid, Beijing and Shanghai. We have Venice and Milan on one side, and Rome on the other. However, the entrepreneurial nature of "trading" cities and the backward-looking bureaucratic nature of political capitals has nothing to do with geography. Rulers chose these locations knowing that information traveled more slowly to, and people had greater difficulty escaping from, landlocked places that were not on trade routes. This left the people working there dependent on political favors. Rulers could exercise far more power over the immobile inhabitants of isolated political capitals.

NO IDEOLOGY, PLEASE

Yet even though political life explains why some countries fell behind and others jumped ahead, that does not mean that we have to get into ideological debates about abstractions such as "freedom" or "government." Freedom means having options. We are "free to choose" when we have alternatives. But alternatives come from having access to capital, from being able to borrow against imagined futures. In the absence of democratized capital markets, "freedom" is an empty word. It may be granted in pieces of paper called constitutions, but when there are no checks and balances, no accountability and dispersion of financial powers, the term has no practical meaning.

And if there is no point engaging in grandiose philosophizing about freedom, there is no point devising grandiose theories about government. Government is a monopolistic financial intermediary that makes decisions about taxation, borrowing, spending, ownership of resources, and granting monopolies. Instead of financiers, politicians and bureaucrats decide how to match money and people.

One of the questions asked in this book is how do we make our politicians and bureaucrats more accountable. The answer offered was to encourage the democratization of capital markets and a greater reliance on the twin pillars of direct democracy—referenda and initiatives—at all levels of government. These institutions would lead to a bottom-up decision on just how "big" a government people want, and how people want their government to spend their money. The trend toward citizen initiative, which we examined in detail in chapter four, continues. In the U.S. elections in November 2000, the following issues were on state ballots: private-school vouchers (in Michigan and California), the repeal of state taxes (in Montana and South Dakota), an across-the-board state tax cut (in Massachusetts), and background checks on buyers at gun shows (in Colorado and Oregon).

Indeed, the democratization of financial markets and the adoption of the institutions of direct democracy are, in my opinion, the keys to lasting prosperity. Places that have adopted them have not only quickly corrected mistaken policies, but also avoided potentially disastrous abuses of power. The mistakes corrected were in the realm of both business and ideas, as the chapters on science, education, and nationalism show.

Open financial markets and direct democracy do not prevent mistakes, however. No institutions can do that. But their ability to correct mistakes sooner, avert some big blunders to start with, and prevent mistaken ideas from taking dangerous turns has had the combined effect of weakening the grip of politics, ideologies, and jargons that bias thoughts. And since capital markets are about the future—market values reflect expectations of future profits from a venture or an idea—they have given rise to societies living in the future. Those societies that have kept their capital markets closed are still living mainly in the past, busily settling the balance sheets of history. Their ability to borrow against the future is limited.

But what is the path from closed to open financial markets? Since the latter disperse power (and the establishment never cedes power voluntarily and politely), is there a way to go from one to the other while avoiding bankruptcy and turmoil? This book shows which paths do not work. Top-down reforms—for example, writing new constitutions while still funneling money through the elites —are a recipe for instability. Indeed, forcing countries to pursue this path has probably been the biggest strategic mistake the West has made in its negotiations with "emerging" countries from Russia to Yasser Arafat's new Palestinian authority. What the West should have done, and should do now, is insist, as a condition of receiving Western capital, that these countries open up their financial markets. The result would be bottom-up reforms, as well as demands for property rights and economic liberties. With closed capital markets, these remain abstractions—even if constitutions make reference to them. Once capital markets are democratized, however, the demands for collateral bring the twin notions of property rights and economic liberties down to earth. People prosper, and disputes are more likely to be settled through negotiation instead of bloody upheavals.

When capital markets are closed, people turn real issues into moral and ideological ones. This should not come as a surprise. If people have limited access to capital, they will turn to family, crime, or government. If family is the source of capital, the transactions are enforced with appeals to morality, religion, custom, and tradition. When government is the source, ideologies and "grand theories" rationalize the roles. In both cases, the societies in question, having limited ability to borrow against the future, live mainly in the past and the present. And backward-looking societies stay poor: they are buried in the act of balancing accounts. They do so because tradition, religion, and custom are the institutions sustaining the few financial transactions that do take place.

Closed capital markets thus have the effect of freezing society. Those who happened to be on the top will stay there, becoming richer through the magic of compound interest. The top will eventually be threatened, however, when those on the bottom begin to observe both the mobility and the riches of more open societies. The establishment, to diffuse the threat and diminish the revolutionary ardor, will occasionally throw a bone to the masses. That's what Otto von Bismarck did in the 1870s when he introduced social security and other "social" benefits—institutions we still live with today. For those in power, providing access to capital through government "benevolence"—and Bismarck admitted explicitly that this was his goal—is a good way to diminish the chances of revolutionary upheaval.

Inequality provokes revolutionary ardor in societies with closed capital markets because people are frozen at the level into which they were born. In societies with open capital markets, however, the poor can move up, and those who do not can hope that their children will. In chapter one, we saw statistics on how many penniless immigrants come to the U.S. and, within a generation, join the *Forbes* 400 list. Or let's consider some numbers from the University of Michigan Panel Survey on Income Dynamics, which tracked the prosperity of more than three thousand people between 1975 and 1991. Only 5 percent of those who were at the bottom in 1975 were still there in 1991. Ninety-five percent had moved up, with more than 50 percent reaching the middle-class quintiles and 29 percent climbing into the top 2 percent. Mobility in the distribution of wealth is what matters, and that mobility is a consequence of open capital markets.

Societies have long been positioned along a wide spectrum, with the United States at one end and nations with closed capital markets—Communist ones included—at the other. Inequality under Communism was as great as, if not greater than, that in other societies. The Communist leaders and party members lived in relative splendor, with free access to the West and Western products. Not surprisingly, envy, malice, suspicion, resentment, and revenge characterized these societies. Inequality provokes such sentiments in societies with open capital markets too. But there, the prospect of mobility sustains hopes and turns envy into either ambition or, occasionally, legitimate channels of limited destruction (such as violating antitrust laws or making false accusations of insider trading, as we saw in chapter one).

But overall, the middle classes have been a stabilizing force. They insured themselves to keep from falling behind, and many of their members bet on a variety of ventures to move up. And if they themselves did not succeed, they made sure their kids would do better. It is this group that has been the catalyst for so much wealth creation. If we block their ability to finance their ventures—by allowing politically motivated financial intermediation —the middle class as a whole will fall behind. The most talented citizens will quit for shores more open to ambition, or they will lower their aspirations and compromise. In both cases, the home country loses.

In such circumstances, those middle-class citizens who remain become dependent on the goodwill of political masters; they become querulous, splintered, a collection of minorities and victims mired in petty envy. When 50 percent of the money in a country flows through government's monopolistic hands, people organize into groups to get a share, and this is often accompanied by rising envy. For the greater the role of government, the more suspicious people become of the success of others. With so much money flowing through government hands, those who are successful likely became so not because of talent, but because of political ties. The result is not a stabilizing middle class, but a frustrated one.

INVESTOR CAPITALISM

The democratization of capital has also brought about changes beyond the rapid distribution of wealth. Because capital is given to talented people to experiment in a wide variety of fields, including engineering, computers, the Internet, biotech, entertainment, media, financial services, and so forth, politicians can no longer count on a stable groups of constituents for support. When sources of capital were limited, politicians could rely on support from immobile farmers, as well as unionized steel and car workers, whose industries seemed stable. But as new industries suddenly appear, others quickly become obsolete—taking once reliable constituencies with them. No wonder American political strategists now recommend targeting stable "niches." Unfortunately, this strategy will not work either, though for a different reason: investor capitalism.

More and more people have diversified assets, and more than 50 percent of U.S. citizens now hold stocks. All these financial assets reflect the value of future earnings streams, and they exceed the GNP by roughly a factor of four. And such widespread ownership of financial assets has additional drastic political consequences. Here is why.

At the beginning of President Bill Clinton's administration, grand plans to increase the federal government's role in health care brought on a $50 billion decline in the market value of companies linked to that industry. When Prime Minister Tony Blair and President Clinton recently promised vaguely to keep future genetic discoveries in the "commons," the market value of companies involved in such research, such as Celera, dropped sharply. Antitrust authorities pursuing Microsoft had a chilling effect not only on that company, but also on a number of others in the field. These examples all show how private stockholders are now directly affected by public policy through market fluctuations. The impact will only increase as the percentage of people holding stocks grows.

Private investors will pay far more attention to the links between stock and bond prices and political agendas. Stock prices have always been susceptible to such fluctuations, of course, but the drops in the past had less public resonance, since only a small minority was immediately affected. When most U.S. citizens had real estate as the main asset in their portfolios, economists had to struggle long and hard to prove the connections between public policy and market performance. This is no longer the case today; links can be traced immediately.

This also helps explain the strong reaction many U.S. politicians have to the idea of privatizing social security. If people are allowed to invest their hard-earned money as they wish, this will diminish significantly the amount of money flowing through the federal intermediary, which will in turn significantly diminish Washington's power. And it will get even worse for the political class. A broad-based ownership of financial assets makes the effects of regulatory and fiscal loopholes, or "tax the rich" platforms, instantly visible. This will make voters more restrained in their support of "special interest" legislation. Thus combining investor capitalism with direct democracy is an additional institutional recipe for prosperity.

At the moment, the United States has gone further toward investor capitalism than other countries. As noted, 56 percent of Americans now hold stocks, a significant increase from the 28 percent who held stocks in 1989. Other countries are catching up, however. Germany has about half a million new investors a year now, for a total of about 5 million in a population of 81 million. South Korea had 2 to 3 million investors ten years ago, and the market was closed to foreigners. Today, there are 7 million in a country of 46 million people, and foreigners own roughly 29 percent of all Korean stocks. In China, the number of investors has jumped from roughly 5 million in 1995 to 55 million today. The government there is encouraging such investment, perhaps because it realizes that stock markets can allocate capital better than debt-laden banks. It would be a stretch to say that China's capital markets are deep, however. Currently, the Chinese refer to the buying and selling of stocks as the "stir-fry market." Players flip stocks within two to six months.

Indirectly, democratized capital markets bring unexpected solutions to many problems. Let's consider, for a moment, the criminal and environmental problems associated with large cities such as Mexico City or Bangkok. Why did 20 million people—20 percent of Mexico's population—end up in one city? Cash flow. Mexico is a federal state in principle, but not in practice. Individual states can retain only 4 percent of the revenue earned from taxes; the rest flows to the federal government in Mexico City. If taxing power was reallocated to the states and capital markets opened, the population would disperse, and criminal and environmental problems would be mitigated.

CHANGE LANGUAGE OF POLITICAL DISCOURSE

When he was asked to identify his biggest academic blunder, Milton Friedman mentioned his efforts in the early 1970s to find a common language with Keynesians. To achieve this goal, he compromised and, as he himself admitted, naively thought that "putting ideas in Keynesian language would put a dent on the Keynesians."

Sometimes it is a mistake to even try to translate one's views into a "customary" jargon. Friedman tried and—predictably—he failed. What he should have realized is that there is no common ground between the language that describes his view of the world and the one that describes the Keynesian vision. Keynesians, and those in favor of centralization, assume that politicians and bureaucrats know exactly what is happening in a society. This assumption is never stated explicitly, but the unaccountable language of "government investing" implies that the "political few" have the solutions to all of society's problems.

The other view—the one represented by Friedman—acknowledges that no one really knows much, but that through trial and error, people have stumbled (and continue to stumble) onto certain rules and institutions that help societies both experiment and correct mistakes when those experiments go awry. The first view uses the language of certainty and arithmetic, the second of uncertainty, possibilities, probabilities, and chance.

The first view, the centralist one, describes the world in terms of the wisdom of the few. The second describes it in terms of the wisdom of the many. The first starts with conditions that represent the complicated state of the world, conditions defined by complex customs, traditions, and institutions. A few "wise men" claim to have identified stable relationships between such conditions, which then can be used to devise policy. The other approach—the one pursued here—looks only at some simple, universal laws of movement that determine people's deviations from them. There is no way anyone can find a common language between these two viewpoints.

In one of his plays, Tom Stoppard has this to say about the misuse of words: "Words don't deserve that kind of malarkey. They're innocent, neutral, precise, standing for this, describing that, meaning the other, so if you look after them you can build bridges across incomprehension and chaos. But when they get their corners knocked off, they're not good any more. . . . I don't think writers are sacred, but words are. They deserve respect. If you get the right ones in the right order, you can nudge the world a little."

There are other reasons for using the language of everyday life when dealing with the business of everyday life, as this book does. As we saw, though there are some general "laws of movement" that help us understand why some societies failed and others prospered, there is no simple correlation between taxes, regulations, and state ownership of certain activities and political institutions. They are the outcome of a unique confluence of personalities and events, international ones in particular. It takes a concrete language to describe uniqueness too.

And there is more to the importance of words and language. Governments around the world today are partly the product of the principle that limiting access to capital markets is the means by which groups can stay in power. But they are also partly the result of responses to centuries of specific crises. When responding to crises, politicians try to remedy the situation with further interventions. Occasionally, the intervention cancels the effect of earlier mistakes. Historians and economists then use this to "prove" that without government regulation, markets would fail. The fact that political and monetary misjudgment and mismanagement created the original crisis is often forgotten. This helps bias thoughts, and lets people fall into what the historian Jonathan Hughes called the "governmental habit" as a chosen solution.

Here is a last, recent example of this. In 1997, Alan Greenspan received the Adam Smith Award from the Association of Private Enterprise Education. In accepting the award, he gave a talk suggesting that private banking has been better for people than one regulated by government. Greenspan backed his claim with a detailed history of American banking. According to his analysis, government regulations were established in response to panics, which often were more perceived than real. Once introduced, the regulations displaced well-structured private arrangements and had unexpected consequences, which then required additional remedies. Nevertheless, the general view was that without government regulation, the crises would have been aggravated.

One would have thought that Greenspan's message would have been widely discussed. But nothing happened. We can speculate on the reason: Greenspan's analysis does not at all fit the viewpoint that permeates the language of political discourse today.

Yogi Berra is credited with saying that if you don't know where you are going, you will end up somewhere else. I would like to add a twist to this and say that you won't know where you are and what hit you unless you know where you came from. To prevent future hits, a clear language must come first.

WHAT NEXT?

So how can other countries catch up if the United States is so far ahead? Well, nothing and nobody is perfect. The United States has its share of bad laws, outdated regulations, complex taxes, and controls inherited from the past, and many of these are still unquestioned. It has bureaucracies whose role is to manage problems, not solve them. These are the things that make it possible for other countries to catch up. What if, for example, the new Russian president, Vladimir Putin, carries out his promise to impose a 13 percent flat tax, a strategy strongly supported by a *New York Times* editorial? With such a simple policy change, Russia would quickly prosper, attracting critical masses of talent and capital, reducing corruption, and leapfrogging over many other countries. Of course, I would not hold my breath waiting for this to happen. But it is an example of a policy that would put a country on the fast track to prosperity. It can be done.

And what if Mexico turned itself into a true federal state, simplified its regulations, and enforced property rights? Part of the Mexican diaspora in the United States would return, and many retired American citizens would move there too, rapidly transferring their know-how to the younger generation. Mexico, a country blessed with natural beauty, a good climate, and great tourist attractions, could soon surpass Florida and Hawaii. Indeed, the country's new president, Vicente Fox, has a golden opportunity to surprise the world and actually exploit Mexico's underutilized location.

If the developed countries want to sustain and even increase the prosperity they've enjoyed in the past two decades, while also helping the rest of the world to prosper, they must turn the next century into a financial one. They must use their negotiating powers and impose narrowly defined mandates on the IMF and the World Bank. The primary goals should be to establish monetary standards, open up financial markets, and recommend fiscal policies that will increase mobility within the distribution of wealth. Constitutions and bureaucracies should be left for later. People should be given a stake in their own society first, for this will further democratize capital markets at home. And the democratization of capital markets will allow people to commercialize more quickly the technological innovations of the past few decades, which in turn will provide the means to fight poverty and disease around the world. The U.S. has gone further in this direction than any other society.

In 1947, in his Iron Curtain speech, Winston Churchill said, "The United States stands at this time at the pinnacle of world power. It is a solemn moment for the American democracy. For primacy in power is also joined in inspiring accountability for the future." These words are perhaps even truer today than when they were spoken half a century ago. Let's hope that the leaders of America will learn to leverage this strength.

SELECT BIBLIOGRAPHY

Amsden, Alice. *Asia's Next Giant: South Korea and Late Industrialization.*
New York: Oxford University Press, 1991.

Bairoch, Paul. *Cities and Economic Development: From the Dawn
of History to the Present.* Chicago: University of Chicago
Press, 1988.

Barbour, Violet. *Capitalism in Amsterdam in the Seventeenth Century.*
Ann Arbor: University of Michigan Press, 1966.

Bartley, Robert L. *The Seven Fat Years.* New York: The Free Press, 1995.

Berman, Harold. *Law and Revolution.* Cambridge, Mass.: Harvard University
Press, 1983.

Bork, Robert. *The Tempting of America: The Political Seduction of the Law.*
New York: The Free Press, 1990.

Brenner, Reuven. *Betting on Ideas: Wars, Invention, Inflation.* Chicago:
University of Chicago Press, 1985.

———. "Canadian Choices." In Boadway, R., T. Courchene, and D. Purvis, eds.

Economic Dimensions of Constitutional Change. Kingston, Ont.: John
Deutsch Institute, 1991.

———. "Canadian Lessons for Euroland." *Forbes Global,* 22 Feb. 1999.

———. "Capital Markets and Democracy." *Journal of Applied
Corporate Finance* (Winter 1999): 66–75.

———. "Comments on Robert Barro's 'Economic Growth,
Convergence, and Government Policies.'" In Zycher, Benjamin,
and Lewis C. Solmon, eds. *Economic Policy, Financial Markets and Economic Growth.* San Francisco: Westview Press, 1993.

———. "Extracting Sunbeams Out of Cucumbers." *Queen's Quarterly*
(Fall 1991): 519–53.

———. "Government and Culture." *Wall Street Journal,* 27 Feb. 1997.

———. *History: The Human Gamble.* Chicago: University of Chicago Press, 1983.

———. *Labyrinths of Prosperity: Economic Follies, Democratic Remedies.*
Ann Arbor: University of Michigan Press, 1994.

———. "The Land of Opportunity." *Forbes Global,* 12 Oct. 1998.

———. "The Long Road from Serfdom, and How to Shorten It." *Canadian Business Law Journal* 17, no. 2 (1990): 195–226.

———. "Making Sense out of Nonsense." In Brenner, Reuven, and David Colander,
eds. *Educating Economists.* Ann Arbor: University of Michigan Press, 1992.

———. "The Makings of an Economic Miracle." *Wall Street Journal,* 5 June 1997.

———. "100 Years of Friedrich Hayek." *Forbes Global,* 17 May 1999.

———. *In Pursuit of Canadian Prosperity.* Montreal: School of Management,
McGill University, 1995.

———. *Rivalry: In Business, Science, among Nations.* Cambridge: Cambridge
University Press, 1989.

———. "What Makes Cities Great?" *Asia Times,* Nov. 1997.

———. "Why Society Needs 'Irrational Exuberance'—and What This Means for
Valuations and Monetary Policy." *Journal of Applied Corporate Finance*
(Summer 2000): 112–18.

———. "Why Stocks Boom and Bust." *Dow Jones Markets* (1996): 31–33.

Brenner, Reuven, and Gabrielle Brenner. *Gambling and Speculation: A
Theory, a History and a Future of Some Human Decisions.* Cambridge:
Cambridge University Press, 1990.

Broder, David. *Democracy Derailed: Initiative Campaigns and the Power of
Money.* New York: Harcourt Brace, 2000.

Coase, Ronald H. *Essays on Economics and Economists.* Chicago: University
of Chicago Press, 1994.

———. *The Firm, the Market and the Law.* Chicago: University of Chicago Press, 1988.

Cohen, Linda R., and Roger G. Noll. *The Technology Pork Barrel.*
Washington D.C.: The Brookings Institute, 1991.

Das, Gurcharan. "Indians Get Ahead." *Wall Street Journal,* 14 Aug. 1997.

——. "A Survey of Cities." Supplement to *The Economist,* 29 July 1995.

Febvre, Lucien. *The Problem of Unbelief in the Sixteenth Century: The
Religion of Rabelais.* Beatrice Gottlieb, trans. Cambridge, Mass.:
Harvard University Press, 1982.

Fitch, B. "The Dutch Masters." *World Business,* Nov./Dec. 1995.

Friedman, Milton, and Anna J. Schwartz. *A Monetary History of the United
States, 1867–1960.* Princeton: Princeton University Press, 1963.

Fukuyama, Francis. *The End of History and the Last Man.* New York:
The Free Press, 1992.

Gibney, Frank. *The Pacific Century.* New York: Scribner's, 1992.

Gleick, James. *Chaos.* New York: Penguin Books, 1987.

Hanke, H. Steve, Lars Jonung, and Kurt Schuler. *Russian Currency and
Finance: A Currency Board Approach to Reform.* London and New York:
Routledge, 1994.

Hayek, Friedrich A. *The Counter-Revolution.* Indianapolis: Liberty Press, 1979.

——. *The Road to Serfdom* (1944). Chicago: University of Chicago Press, 1976.

Hughes, Jonathan. *The Vital Few* (1965). London: Oxford University Press, 1973.

Huntington, Samuel P. *The Clash of Civilization and the Remaking
of World Order.* New York: Simon and Schuster, 1996.

Jacobs, Jane. *Cities and the Wealth of Nations.* New York: Vintage Books,
1985.

Kanter, Rosabeth Moss. "Thriving Locally in the Global Economy."
Harvard Business Review, Sept./Oct. 1995: 151–60.

——. *World Class: Thriving Locally in the Global Economy.* New York: Simon
and Schuster, 1995.

Kedourie, Elie. *Nationalism.* Oxford: Blackwell, 1993.

Kennedy, Paul. *The Rise and Fall of the Great Powers: Economic Change and
Military Conflict from 1500 to 2000.* New York: Random House, 1987.

Keynes, John Maynard. *General Theory of Employment, Interest and Money.*
New York: Harcourt, 1965.

Kotkin, Joel. *Tribes: How Race, Religion and Identity Determine Success in the
New Global Economy.* New York: Random House, 1993.

Krugman, Paul. *The Return of Depression Economics.* New York:
W. W. Norton, 1999.

Kuznets, Simon. *National Income and Its Composition, 1919–1938.*
Washington: National Bureau of Economic Research, 1941.

Landes, David. *The Wealth and Poverty of Nations: Why Some Are So Rich and Some So Poor.* New York: W. W. Norton, 1998.

Mandeville, Bernard de. *The Fable of the Bees* (1714). New York: Capricorn Books, 1962.

McNeill, William. *The History of Western Civilization: A Handbook.* Chicago: University of Chicago Press, 1986.

———. *Polyethnicity and National Unity in World History.* Toronto: University of Toronto Press, 1986.

———. *The Pursuit of Power.* Chicago: University of Chicago Press, 1982.

———. *The Rise of the West.* Chicago: University of Chicago Press, 1963.

Mundell, Robert A. *Monetary Theory.* Pacific Palisades, Calif.: Goodyear Publishing, 1971.

Needham, J. *Science and Civilisation in China* (1954). Cambridge: Cambridge University Press, 1961.

Ohmae, Kenichi. *The Borderless World: Power and Strategy in the Interlinked Economy.* Toronto: HarperCollins, 1991.

Peterson, Peter. *Gray Dawn.* New York: Times Books, 1999.

Popper, Karl. *The Open Society and Its Enemies.* London: Routledge, 1945.

Reich, Robert. *The Work of Nations: Preparing Ourselves for Twenty-first Century Capitalism.* Toronto: Random House, 1991.

Rosecrance, Richard. *The Rise of the Trading State.* New York: Basic Books, 1986.

Schama, Simon. *Citizens: A Chronicle of the French Revolution.* New York: Knopf, 1991.

Schlesinger, Arthur Jr. "Has Democracy a Future?" *Foreign Affairs* 76, no. 5 (Sept./Oct. 1997): 2–13.

Schumpeter, Joseph A. *The Economics and Sociology of Capitalism.* Edited by R. Swedberg. Princeton: Princeton University Press, 1991.

Shelton, Judy. *The Coming Soviet Crash.* New York: The Free Press, 1989.

Smith, Adam. *The Wealth of Nations* (1776). Chicago: University of Chicago Press, 1976.

Tocqueville, Alexis de. *Democracy in America* (1835). Edited and abridged by Richard D. Heffner. New York: New American Library, 1956.

Wanniski, Jude. *The Way the World Works: How Economies Fail and Succeed* (1978). Morristown, N.J.: Polyconomics, 1989.

Wolfe, Tom. *From Bauhaus to Our House.* New York: Farrar, Straus and Giroux, 1981.

Wriston, Walter. *The Twilight of Sovereignty: How the Information Revolution Is Transforming Our World.* New York: Simon and Schuster, 1992.

INDEX

bonds, 27, 47, 114, 117, 120, 123. *See also* junk bonds
Bork, Robert, 172–73
borrowing, 10, 12, 25, 37, 83.
See also loans
Botero, Giovanni, 88
Bourbon, Nicolas, 169
brain drain, 29, 75, 198
Brazil, 3, 17, 23, 59, 64, 120, 128,
bribery, 15, 22, 46, 54, 75, 147.
See also corruption
Britain. *See* United Kingdom
Broder, David, 97, 99
bureaucracies, 59, 63, 91–92, 94, 129, 147, 186, 205, 206.
See also individual countries

Cambridge University, 181
Cameroon, 64–65, 149
Canada, 2–3, 45, 84, 148–49.
See also dollar, Canadian; Quebec
brain drain from, 29, 75
inflationary targets in, 109–10
natural resources in, 2, 52
ownership in, 34, 67
referenda in, 100–1
taxation in, 29, 149
workforce in, 68, 102
capital, 2–3, 9, 18, 21, 80, 109. *See also* capital markets
access to, 24, 35–36, 54–55, 98–99, 196
government as source of, 2, 9, 11, 12
human, 3, 71
and science, 156–59
capital gains. *See* taxes
capitalism, 12, 18, 21–23, 27, 38, 63, 201–203
Capitalism: The Unknown Ideal (Greenspan), 112–13
capital markets, 3, 16, 24, 30, 76–77, 123, 194–95. *See also* individual countries;

capitalism
access to, 9–11, 201
closed, 3, 10–11, 24, 36, 148, 166, 198, 20–03
and culture, 24–25
and democracy, 3–4, 12–13, 16, 27, 34–36
democratization of, 25, 144, 200–02, 204, 206
and elites, 5, 33
cargo cults, 22–23, 38, 63, 190, 192
Carnegie Mellon University, 177, 180
casinos. *See* gambling
caste systems, 62
centralization, 15–16, 141, 146–47, 149, 207–208
change, political, 3, 104, 204, 206
Chavez, Hugo, 23–24
checks and balances. *See* accountability
China, 16–17, 29, 60, 66, 68, 70, 159, 199, 206.
See also Hong Kong
emigration from, 68, 77, 198
Churchill, Winston, 117, 210
civil rights, 148, 183
Cleveland, Grover, 114–15
Clinton, Bill, 205
Coase, Ronald, 155–56
Cohen, Linda, 93–94
Cold War, 97. *See also* Communism
collateral. *See* borrowing
Columbia University, 155, 196
Common Market, 72–73. *See also* European Community
communication, 83, 97, 147, 150. *See also* language
Communication Quarterly, 186
Communism, 4, 11–13, 15, 17, 21, 42–43, 65, 58, 144–46, 154, 203. *See also* China; Soviet Union
fall of, 4, 11, 13, 15, 17, 42, 154–155
competition, 11, 16
Confucianism, 159

consumer price index (CPI), 104, 108–9
contracts, 3, 5, 22, 55, 63–64, 198
and macroeconomics, 26–27
money and, 104, 116–20, 123–24, 126, 129–30
and prices, 113–15
convergence, 198–99
Copernicus, 158
Cornell University, 180, 196
corporations, 27–28
corruption, 12, 15, 22, 65, 81, 201. *See also* bribery
Cowperthwaite, John, 39
credit, 27–28
access to, 22, 30, 36, 41, 73, 101–102
crime, 19, 51
as political response, 3, 10, 202
as source of capital, 11, 19–20, 197, 202
culture, 24–26, 47–50, 90, 141, 147–48, 150
currency, 107–8, 121. *See also* currency boards; gold standard
crises in, 36, 64, 102, 104–6, 113–14, 117, 122–24, 125
and trust, 25–28, 104, 128
volatility of, 6, 104, 108, 122–23
currency boards, 6, 27, 106, 108, 112, 124
Czechoslovakia, 17, 71, 143

Debreu, Gerard, 157
debt, 25, 26, 41, 44, 59, 65, 76. *See also* borrowing, loans
decentralization. *See* centralization
default, 40–44, 90, 119, 123
defence, 61–62. *See also* military
deficits, 44, 81–82, 84, 105,
deflation, 19, 106, 113–14, 116,
DeLong, Brad, 118–19

Taxes (*continued*):
  capital gains, 47–48,
    110, 126–27
  and direct democracy,
    94–95
  and education, 173,
    190–92
  flat, 55–56, 208–9
  government use of, 9,
    37, 83
  income, 21, 55, 71, 74,
    98
  and mobility, 62, 101,
    133, 206
  simplifying, 55–58
  value-added, 91
Taylor rule, 107
technology, 126, 158, 198
  and education, 177
  and mobility, 30, 62, 63,
    77, 97, 177
tenure, 65, 179, 181,
  185–86, 191–92
Thailand, 34, 59, 63, 104
Thatcher, Margaret, 21, 34
Tito (Josip Broz), 146
Tocqueville, Alexis de, 38,
  140
Tonegawa, Susumu, 163
trade, 60–61, 67, 115,
  210, 134, 199
Treaty of Versailles, 19,
  71
tribalism. *See* nationalism
Trudeau, Pierre, 149
Trump, Donald, 50
trust, 6–7, 25–26, 103,
  140, 144–48
  and capital markets, 4,
    13, 15, 26, 63, 133, 197
Tschudi, Aegidius, 134
Tuchman, Barbara, 171
Tudjman, Franjo, 146
tuition fees, 178, 193
Turkey, 16, 24, 36, 141
Tytler, Alexander Fraser,
  40–44

unemployment, 18–19,
  43, 52, 55, 84–88,
  101, 114, 121. *See
  also* poverty
United Kingdom, 21, 29,
  40, 43, 66, 70, 72,

103, 110, 160, 197.
  See also pound sterling
  gold standard in, 114,
    117–19
  government roles in, 18,
    31, 114, 175
  and Scotland, 30, 41–72
United Nations, 29, 92,
  144, 165
United States, 1–3, 12,
  18–19, 27, 31–34, 45,
  47, 78, 92, 97, 98,
  100–01, 105, 111,
  114, 162, 175–76,
  194, 199, 203, 206,
  209–10 . *See also*
  dollar, American
  accountability in, 31, 45
  direct democracy in,
    97–101
  education in, 175 194
  election issues in, 45,
    92, 199
  and entrepreneurs,
    27–30, 68
  gold standard in,
    111–14, 118
  government policies of,
    32, 92, 170, 175,
    203
  immigration to, 59, 76,
    94, 203
  international role of, 12,
    18, 121, 126, 131,
    143, 151
  investors in, 51, 206
  mistakes in, 31, 45, 53
  privatization in, 32, 47
  prosperity in, 2, 25,
    27–31, 77, 207
  taxation in, 93, 97–98,
    112, 207
  workforce in, 18, 70
universities, 161, 170,
  176, 183. *See also*
  individual universities
  economics as taught by,
    154, 171
  pressures on, 177
  private, 175, 179, 181,
    194
  subsidies for, 169, 175
  virtual, 178
University of Berlin, 196

University of California,
  177, 179
University of Michigan,
  203
University of Phoenix,
  178
U.S. Bureau of Labor
  Statistics, 193
USSR. *See* Soviet Union
usury laws, 30, 62

Valley-Radot, René, 168
value, 76, 81, 129. *See
  also* devaluation
Venezuela, 3, 17, 21,
  23–24, 64
venture capital, 25,
  28–29, 83
volatility, 6
votes. *See* elections

Wall Street Journal, 112,
  123, 153–155, 171
Wanniski, Jude, 112
wars, 17, 68, 86, 101,
  137, 139, 141, 144,
  190
Warwick University, 181
waste management, 175
Waters, Dane, 98
wealth, 64, 203. *See also*
  prosperity
  redistribution of, 34, 35,
    39, 55, 210
Weber, Max, 25
welfare, 51, 88. *See also*
  poverty
welfare state, 102
Wilson, Woodrow, 132,
  144, 147
Wolfe, Tom, 170–71
Wood, N. R., 167
World Bank, 65, 210
Wriston, Walter, 123
Wynn, Steven, 49

Yang, Jerry, 28
Yeltsin, Boris, 100–01
yen, 104, 110
Yugoslavia. *See* Balkan
  states

Zaire, 3, 23, 64–65

About TEXERE

TEXERE seeks to become the most progressive and authoritative voice in business publishing by cultivating and enhancing ideas that will illuminate the global business landscape. Our name defines the spirit of our vision: TEXERE is the ancient Latin verb "to weave." In an increasingly global business community, we seek to create an intersection where authors and readers can share the best thinking and the latest ideas. We want to leverage the expertise and insights of leading thinkers by weaving them with TEXERE's capability to deliver them to the marketplace.

To learn more and become a part of our community, visit us at:
www.etexere.com
and
www.etexere.co.uk

About the Typeface
This book was set in *Sabon*